WOOD &
Glory

Dear: Mr. Calley

We wanted to present this book to you as a token of our appreciation. Thank you so much for your business over the years! Your support has allowed us to continually grow since 2003, and provide you with the assistance you need at your cottage. We hope you have enjoyed your season in Muskoka, and look forward to working with you again next year!

Sincerely,

Loon Call

BENNETT CARTER

Abigail Van Den Broek

DAVID NABER

MUSKOKA'S CLASSIC LAUNCHES

WOOD & *Glory*

William M. Gray

Photography by Timothy C. Du Vernet

The BOSTON
MILLS PRESS

A BOSTON MILLS PRESS BOOK

PUBLISHED BY BOSTON MILLS PRESS
132 Main Street, Erin, Ontario, Canada N0B 1T0
Tel 519-833-2407   Fax 519-833-2195
e-mail: books@bostonmillspress.com
www.bostonmillspress.com

In Canada:
DISTRIBUTED BY FIREFLY BOOKS LTD.
66 Leek Crescent, Richmond Hill, Ontario, Canada L4B 1H1

In the United States:
DISTRIBUTED BY FIREFLY BOOKS (U.S.) INC.
P.O. Box 1338, Ellicott Station
Buffalo, New York, USA 14205

NATIONAL LIBRARY OF CANADA CATALOGUING IN PUBLICATION

Gray, W. M. (William Melville), 1953-
Wood & glory : Muskoka's classic launches / William M. Gray ;
photography by Timothy C. Du Vernet.

ISBN 1- 55046-177-X (bound)   ISBN 1-55046-419-1 (pbk.)

1. Wooden boats--Ontario--Muskoka--History.
2. Wooden boats--Ontario--Muskoka--Pictorial works.
3. Launches--Ontario--Muskoka--History.
4. Launches--Ontario--Muskoka--Pictorial works.
I. Du Vernet, Tim II. Title. III. Title: Wood and glory.

VM341.G72 1997   623.8'2314'0971316   C97-930541-1

PUBLISHER CATALOGING-IN-PUBLICATION DATA (U.S.)

Gray, W. M. (William Melville), 1953-
Wood & glory : Muskoka's classic launches / William M. Gray ;
photography by Timothy C. Du Vernet.
[ ] p. : col. ill. ;   cm.

ISBN 1- 55046-419-1 (pbk.)

1. Launches -- Ontario -- Muskoka (District municipality)
-- History.
2. Launches -- Ontario -- Muskoka (District municipality)
-- Pictorial works.
3. Wooden boats -- Ontario -- Muskoka (District municipality)
-- History.
4. Wooden boats -- Ontario -- Muskoka (District municipality)
-- Pictorial works.
5. Boatbuilding -- Ontario -- Muskoka (District municipality)
-- History. I. Du Vernet, Timothy C. II. Title.

623.8207/ 09713   VM341.G734 2004

The publisher acknowledges for the financial support of our publishing program the Canada Council, the Ontario Arts Council, and the Government of Canada through the Book Publishing Industry Development Program (BPIDP).

Text and cover design by Talyor/Sprules Corporation
Printed in China

CONTENTS

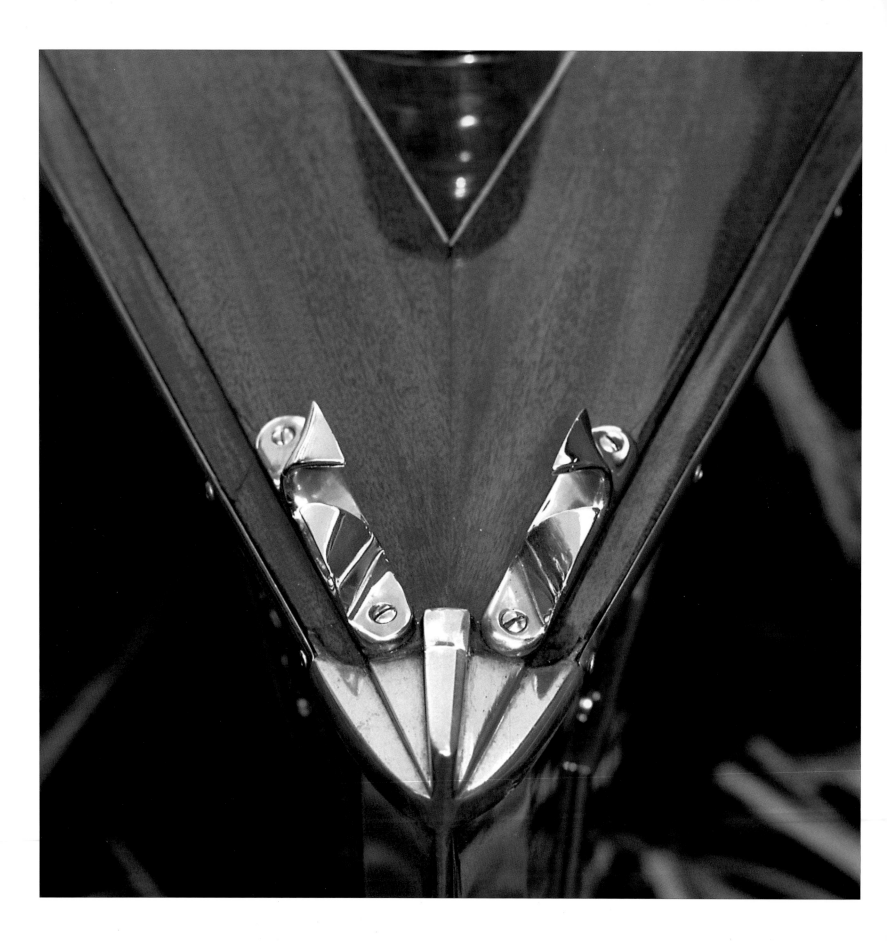

PREFACE

Once upon a time, not so very long ago, the better sort of pleasure boat was built, not manufactured. They were built to order, by hand, of the finest materials — oak, cedar and elm from Ontario; fir from British Columbia; mahogany from the Honduras, the Philippines and the east coast of Africa. Some of the best were built in Ontario, many of them in Muskoka.

This book is about some of those launches, as the old centre-drive displacement boats were known in Muskoka, boats that represent a special era of boating, an era that flowered before the Second World War.

Muskoka boasted a unique concentration of these fine craft for a few reasons. In the late 1800s the region became a major tourist destination for both Canadians and Americans. Gradually, as summer followed summer, many of these tourists decided to purchase land and build cottages on the innumerable islands and points that break the rocky and heavily wooded shoreline of lakes Muskoka, Rosseau and Joseph. Road access to much of the mainland shoreline was quite limited until well after the Second World War, thus large boats were a simple necessity.

Because Muskoka was an international resort area, it was the summer home of a disproportionately high number of people with large disposable incomes. In other words, the many wealthy families who summered here year after year could afford to foster and support a local custom-boat building industry. One only has to look to three or four families on Lake of Bays, and a couple of dozen on the Muskoka Lakes, to find the people who, through their regular patronage, kept many craftsmen in business.

*OPPOSITE: **Norwood II** bow detail.*

Between the wars, the local market was protected by a weak Canadian dollar and a healthy import tariff; Muskoka was also sufficiently distant from the major American factories then mass-producing stock runabouts. In the late 1920s Chris-Craft built in a day as many boats of one design as Ditchburn did of their best-selling model in a year — and Ditchburn was then the largest motorboat builder in Canada.

Most launches on these waters were built by local craftsmen for a local market. Many are "one off" boats reflecting the particular desires of the buyer and the peculiar, uniquely identifiable craftsmanship of the builder.

Classic is one of those rubbery adjectives that means different things to different people. I consider many of the motorboats built between the wars, and some of the custom work done after the Second World War, to be classic, and anything built before the First World War to be antique. Then again, all those Dukes, the Disappearing Propeller Boats (Dispros or Dippies), and the Port Carling Boat Work's SeaBirDs are in a quite different, but still very important sense, also classic Muskoka boats. They constitute a special part of the boating legacy of these waters and, in a broader sense, of our national heritage.

The term is also applied to some marques, the work of certain builders or shops, and many would argue that anything that floated and came from Ditchburn's or Minett's shops is a classic. The "streamliners," or cigar boats as they were popularly called, and the other custom work that came out of Greavette's, as well as the odd surviving launch built by Earl Barnes or Clive Brown, would also fall within that category. In this book I will deal with the issue largely by avoiding any tight definitions. I believe that many very able builders were fostered by the peculiar situation on these lakes.

The waters of the three largest interconnected Muskoka lakes — Muskoka, Rosseau and Joseph — are still home to a large number of classic custom-built wooden launches. A few date back to the early years of this century, some are more contemporary, built as recently as the 1970s, but the great majority exemplify a special era of boating that lasted from 1914 to 1940.

Muskoka is kind to wooden boats. More to the point, the ice in the Muskoka Lakes is kinder to boathouses than is the ice in Georgian Bay, the Kawartha Lakes, or in many of the other resort areas. The traditional boathouse, built over stone-filled wooden crib docks and slips, provides the ideal environment for a wooden boat. The cribs break up the waves and protect the launch from undue motion, and the shelter of the boathouse naturally protects the finish from the sun's rays.

Many of the vintage launches that one finds plying Muskoka waters have seen continuous use since they were first built. They have been a special part of the Muskoka scene for decades. They embody both a unique personality and a living history, and in many cases they are old friends to both the families who own them and to their neighbours on these lakes.

INTRODUCTION

A custom-built wooden boat is the living manifestation of the boatbuilder's art. It is crafted of organic materials and will therefore decay over its lifespan. Each boat possesses individual characteristics that are defined, to a greater or lesser degree, by its designer and by the craftsmen who created it.

Launches can be classified, very generally, into two groups: those with displacement hulls and those with planing hulls. The displacement-hull, or round-bottomed, boat enjoyed its heyday from the earliest days of power boating until the onset of the Great Depression. The V-bottom, hard-chine or planing boats were introduced well before 1920, but did not really gain favour with the general public in Muskoka until the late 1920s, when engines became both powerful and light enough to get the boats up on the water.

OPPOSITE: This aerial view of the Ditchburn plant in the mid-twenties captures the spirit of old Gravenhurst.

To make a general statement about anything concerning the Muskoka motorboat is akin to motoring at full throttle into uncharted waters. Because the hallmark of the boatbuilding industry in Muskoka was the custom-built launch, by definition we are dealing primarily with the exceptions rather than the rules.

In boating's golden days, between the wars, a number of Ontario boatbuilders turned out beautiful wooden boats finished to a high standard: Gilbert in Brockville, Taylor and Sachau in Toronto, Ross in Orillia, Gidley on Georgian Bay, and numerous independents on the different waterways. But very little of their work has survived. The principal shops that built the launches we still admire today were located in Muskoka.

In the 1920s it became popular to talk about standardized runabouts, what we would call stock boats. Shops would build a number of hulls, usually already fitted out with an engine, and have them on hand for immediate sale. Large-scale production reduced costs and lowered retail prices. This was not the case in Muskoka, however. In a some ways the Disappearing Propeller Boat Company in Port Carling attempted to manufacture their models on this principle in the 1920s, and Greavette's was organized to attempt something along these lines in 1930, but the Disappearing Propeller Boat Company failed after a few years, and Greavette's gave up the idea after two consecutive years of severe losses. (In fact, the company didn't make any money for the first nine years of its existence.)

In the United States, in addition to a number of small regional builders, several large factories turned out thousands of excellent stock runabouts that set design and craftsmanship standards for other American builders. Chris-Craft, Gar Wood, Hackercraft, Dart, and Sea Lyon number among the best-known builders of the 1920s and 1930s. There was no comparable large works engaged in the mass production of stock motorboats in Muskoka. It is not that some makers did not try to emulate the production methods of boat industry leaders to the south, they just never made a go of it.

What is the difference between an American-built and a Muskoka-built launch? Well, the quick answer is the simple understatement of the Canadian boat. Before the war, none of Muskoka's principal builders painted his name on the motorboats coming out of his shop. After the war, Greavette marked its stock lines with its name in chrome letters, but before the war, the occasional use of their trademark arrow running down the hull was the limit of their identification. Muskoka-built launches, if identified at all, had a simple, small brass plate on their dash panels to indicate the maker. In the case of a major builder such as Ditchburn, the year and the number of the vessel were included. More often than not, boat enthusiasts could tell where a boat came from by its appearance. Each builder's craft had a look, and each boat possessed individual characteristics that were easily identifiable to those in the know.

The broadest observations concerning the differences between launches built in Muskoka and those built in the United States must start with their respective appearances. The owner-assigned names of centre-drive launches in Muskoka, if

ABOVE: *Clean and classic. The uncluttered, sophisticated deck and hardware on a 26-foot Minett launch.*

that matter. There was less bright work, less chromium-plate trim, less flash, less glitter.

Two-toned decks were popular in the United States but were an oddity on these waters. The dark coverboard with the contrasting lighter or redder deck was something that Greavette played with (at Harold Wilson's instigation) in the mid-thirties and again after the war. (To my mind, this simply tarted up something that should have been left to stand alone — it was sort of like adding fins and tail lights — but then again, it is a matter of personal preference.) It must also be noted that Muskoka boatbuilders used only a yellow composition to caulk deck seams from about 1920.

Boatbuilders in Muskoka generally placed their forward navigation lights close to the stem, while American runabouts featured them much further back on the forward deck. While Greavette adopted the American-style plated cutwater, the other Muskoka builders maintained the traditional practice of using a cast-aluminum stem. Very few launches were fitted with anything but navy tops until well after the Second World War. This style that was a distinct novelty in the United States.

displayed at all, were presented in nickel or chromium-plate letters mounted on the boats' light boxes, the boards set by the navigation lights, just forward of the cockpit. On the forward-drive boats, the names were usually displayed on the hull. No Muskoka boatbuilder painted the name of the boat on the transom, or anywhere else for

ABOVE: Boat shows organized by the Muskoka Lakes Association and the Antique and Classic Boat Society have become summer highlights.

In August 1971 Bob Purves, the Commodore of the Muskoka Lakes Association (M.L.A.), organized the first boat show in Muskoka. This bi-annual gathering has continued to the present day. The 1971 show was held at the Muskoka Lakes Golf and Country Club, but the event has since been moved to the docks at Port Carling. The M.L.A. boat show was the first such gathering in Canada, and at the time, ignorant of the shows organized at Clayton, New York, in the 1960s, it was thought to be the first gathering of classic wooden boats anywhere.

One of those rare people who actually translates dreams into reality, Mr. Purves thought that tribute should be paid to the craftsmen of Muskoka, and in so doing give the people who had always treasured this specific aspect of our Muskoka heritage an opportunity to gather and enjoy the beauties of our collective boating past. Close to a hundred launches, all built before 1940, all very much still in everyday use, some in good condition, some in need of a little tender loving care — or at least another coat of varnish — assembled at the Muskoka Lakes Golf and Country Club that August, and the lake with the greatest representation of boats was presented with a bushel of corn. There were no prizes, no classifications, no nonsense. This spirit still governs the M.L.A. gatherings of wooden boats.

The Antique and Classic Boat Society has been responsible for drawing a great deal of attention to the classic wooden launches and runabouts with their regular organized shows and displays at the Toronto Boat Show. Unlike the M.L.A.'s gatherings, competition has been a primary focus at the A.C.B.S. show, and awards are presented for the best Minett, Ditchburn, and so on. While I suppose there are benefits to this preoccupation with the "best," there are also many drawbacks. Such judging forces square pegs into round holes. The beauty of the boatbuilder's art in Muskoka was the marriage of the interests of the customer and the builder. It still is, for that matter. If the launch did not give satisfaction, it was altered. If the original power plant was not appropriate, it was changed. If the owner decided to modernize his launch and incorporate more of the then fashionable streamlining features, he did it. Authenticity is a dubious yardstick to apply to the custom-built launches of Muskoka. These launches were the owners', not the builders'. They were built to be used. If a launch delivered in 1938 closely resembled a launch built in 1928 but with the "wrong" hardware, so be it, it was what the owner ordered.

But this raises an important question: When does a boat become a reproduction? There is no satisfactory answer. The classic launches from the 1920s and 1930s are all reaching the end of their natural lives. Because they were constructed of organic materials and subject to decay, if parts are not replaced in a timely manner, the result will be an untimely visit to the bottom of the lake over which they once cruised so glamorously. Such an end benefits no one.

The traditional arts of building, repairing and finishing a boat to the standards set by the original builders have been lost in most areas where these arts once flourished. Synthetics replaced natural materials in almost all small boat construction well over thirty years ago. The cost effectiveness of mass production, enhanced by the use of fibreglass and metal in boat construction, brought an end to most of the shops in which boatbuilders still worked with wood.

But traditional boatbuilding is by no means a dead art in Muskoka. There are several builders in the district who remain in business today, and who will gladly undertake a commission to build you a custom launch that will equal, and may well excel, the demanding standards of the past.

EARLY DAYS

One hundred years ago the Muskoka Lakes saw its first boat powered with a gasoline motor. It was a 16-foot launch with a two-cycle engine, purchased by John Moodie from the Sinty Gas Engine Company of Grand Rapids, Michigan. Moodie had bought it in 1895 and, after a season's use on Hamilton Bay, brought it up to Muskoka. In 1930 Hugh Neilson recollected that the second such launch was brought to Muskoka by Reuben Miller, and that he had rides in both boats before he brought the *Wren* to his island in Lake Muskoka in 1902. The *Wren* was a Racine-built launch with a one-cylinder two-cycle Racine engine.

Interest in motorboating burgeoned in the first decade of the twentieth century. The number of shops building gasoline engines and

*OPPOSITE: The newly restored **Wanda III** epitomizes the old private steam yacht, which saw its heyday before the First World War.*

motorboats multiplied each year, parallelling the fascination with new developments in automobiles, and more especially the remarkable advances in the efficiency and dependability of the gasoline engine. The principal boatbuilders who supplied the market in Muskoka in these early years were located in the United States, Toronto and Hamilton.

It is believed that local boatbuilders started building motorboats in 1903, and by the 1930s Muskoka was described as the cradle of motorboating in Canada. Many Muskoka craftsmen built boats — sailboats, rowboats, canoes and scows. Among the most successful builders were the Ditchburns, with shops at Rosseau, Port Carling and Gravenhurst, and the Johnstons, in Port Carling and Port Sandfield. A great many others worked on the lakes during the season, then built a boat or two during the winter. This practice continued into the 1960s.

Early launches powered by gasoline engines were simply small steam launches with an alternative (and it must be said, far less dependable) power plant; and at that, many steam launches resembled nothing so much as small sailing craft that had been adapted to suit steam. Most were relatively small, 16 to 20-odd feet long, with one large open cockpit, and the exposed engine mounted in the middle. They were invariably painted white, with varnished decks planked in oak, or of alternating, contrasting strips of dark and light wood. The larger boats were often fitted with canopies.

Of the three early, locally built, open-cockpit launches that are known to still exist, one is definitely the work of Bert Minett — he said as much to several people — and the two others are now attributed to him. I say this with a degree of caution, as most of the early launches were built by boatbuilders in Toronto or the United States.

In Muskoka, Ditchburn was building on a much larger scale than anyone else, and many other men were turning out small launches each winter. Most of these boats were virtually indistinguishable from each other. Hardware

was bought from merchants in the city, and everyone was kept busy copying what everyone else was doing.

The first Canadian gasoline launches were built in Toronto in 1902; earlier gasoline launches had all come up from the United States. The Canada Launch and Engine Works at the foot of Carlaw Avenue was probably the first in the city, but within a year or two they were in competition with the Leader Bicycle Company on King Street West, the Walter Nicholls Motorboat Company on Wellington Street, and the Toronto Gas and Gasoline Engine Company at the corner of Lake and York. By 1906 there were six boatbuilders in Hamilton who built launches: T.W. Jutten, Jas. Massey, John Morris, Robertson Bros., Jas. Weir & Sons, and H.L. Bastien. Bastien ran boat liveries and sold his launches in Muskoka before the First World War.

John Hendry had been building small boats in Toronto from the late 1880s, and in 1902 his operations were organized as a limited company to manufacture motorboats on a large scale. This new venture was called the Canada Launch Works. Morris M. Whitaker, a highly regarded

Above: This steam launch is typical of the many small boats seen on inland waterways at the turn of the century.

naval architect, was president of the company until 1906. The Canada Launch Works became a hothouse for a number of builders who would go on to make names for themselves. J.J. Taylor, the English-born master boatbuilder who became such a fixture between the wars, with his yard at the bottom of Bathurst Street building cruisers, joined the Canada Launch Works in 1904, and after it was taken over by Schofield Holden, became the master builder.

One of the leading boatbuilders in 1909, M.L. Butler of Brighton, Ontario, was another early employee. Butler sold twenty-nine launches in 1909, and among the orders that he had on his books for 1910 were a number of boats with some startlingly lean dimensions. His speedboat was 25 feet long and had a beam of 3 feet 10 inches. In 1910 a typical 32-foot fast boat had a

*ABOVE: A beautiful example of the first generation of gasoline launches, the 19-foot **Floss** is believed to be an early Minett dating from about 1905.*

*BELOW: A typical twin-cylinder engine, this **Buffalo** is thought to generate about 4-horsepower.*

beam of 5 feet; in 1917 the beam was increased to 6 feet; and by 1930 a displacement launch of that length would be built with a beam of 6 feet 6 inches.

The costs of the transportation of a finished motorboat or launch from Toronto or Hamilton to Ontario's resort areas proved a huge boon to local builders. In addition, a great many members of the boat-buying public in Muskoka were from south of the border and were more inclined to look to a local boatbuilder than to a shop in their home country.

Advertising copy from the 1910s suggests that Ditchburn was experimenting with gasoline launches in 1898 (though it is unlikely that his shop actually built them at that time), and that Bert Minett built his first small gasoline launch at Clevelands House in 1903. It is doubtful that anyone built a motorboat in Muskoka before this date.

In 1902 or 1903 Henry Ditchburn made arrangements for his nephew Herb to go to Racine, Wisconsin, to learn something about the building of motorboats. The night before he arrived, the boatworks burnt down. Herb took a job shovelling coal and then as a carpenter in a department store. He subsequently returned to the Ditchburn works in Gravenhurst, where he worked for his Uncle Henry for three years, at which time the business was incorporated and Henry's interest bought out (though he didn't retire until 1910).

The H. Ditchburn Boat Manufacturing Company Ltd. was incorporated in June 1907 with a charter to manufacture gasoline boats. The first directors of the new venture were Herb and Alf Ditchburn and Tom Greavette, of whom a great deal will be heard later.

In 1908 Ditchburn introduced a "speed boat" that was 27 by 4 1/2 feet. The front deck was 6 feet and the "hood" 5 feet in length. The frames and keel were made from white oak, it was planked and decked in Ontario cedar, and the covering boards and coaming were mahogany. The interior detailing was offered in either cedar or mahogany, and with the finer lines and lighter weight than their earlier work, it was advertised that the boat was capable of 20 miles per hour.

The point was made that most speedboats were "cranky and wet" but that with this new

caulked and payed with black marine glue. The deck fittings were polished brass. I was once told that before the First World War some local builders adopted the practice of caulking the deck seams with "yellow composition" instead of black, after seeing an American boat done this way, presumably after mahogany became a popular decking material, about 1910. Others continued to use the traditional method of filling the seams with narrow strips of spruce until the early twenties. While it was to remain the standard with local builders until production ceased in the 1970s, it was by no means the universally accepted method south of the border.

Between 1908 and 1910 the earliest recognizable versions of what was to become

Ditchburn design, with an "inverted wedge type" hull, coupled with a marked flare out from the waterline to the gunwale, the spray would be thrown out as much as possible and prevent it from breaking over the deck when at speed. A 9-to-10-horsepower engine would make 14 miles per hour; a 12-to-18-horsepower engine, 16 miles per hour; and an 18-to-20-horsepower engine, 19 miles per hour.

Their most successful design at that time was a 28-foot launch, introduced in 1905. Decks were clear white spruce, mahogany or cherry,

ABOVE: Brass and kerosene were readily abandoned when nickel plate and electricity became available.

*ABOVE OPPOSITE: The Ditchburn-built **Memphis**, shown in these drawings, dates from 1908 or 1909.*

*BELOW OPPOSITE: The **Memphis** at the 1909 Muskoka Lakes Association Motor Boat races just outside Port Carling.*

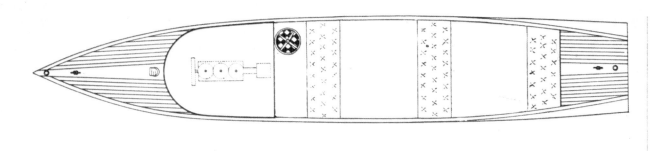

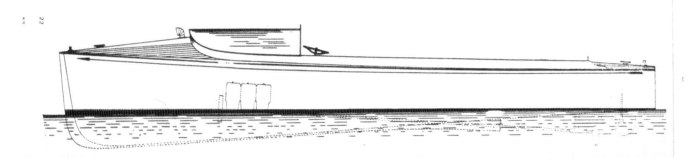

for a metal stem in 1912, and almost all the builders in Muskoka followed suit. I believe that Borneman, on Gull Lake, was one builder who continued to use a wooden stem, over which he attached a metal cutwater or sheath to protect the bow of the vessel from small obstructions. Some believe that the use of a metal stem rabetted to take the planks was introduced by A.H. Duke, but the record is not clear.

All the builders used cowl ventilators. These are high-standing engine ventilators that resemble, in miniature, those found on steamers. When the builders started enclosing the engine in a compartment forward of the cockpit, the practice was to place a single ventilator forward of the raised hatch and coaming, but within a few years two were being installed, to either side of the now flush set hatches, or in some instances forward of them.

By 1915 Ditchburn launches sported transom binders that swept forward at the chafing rail, or rub rail, picking up that line as it approached the transom. Minett never used transom binders, though many owners have subsequently had them added to protect the hull at the junction of the hull planking with the transom.

More distance was placed between the motorboat operator and his charge, as more dependable engines required less constant care. Portholes were now set into the engine bulkhead to allow the driver or engineer to keep a watchful eye on what was going on (or not going on) in the engine compartment. And mechanisms were fitted to engines to allow their operators to crank them from behind, through the engine compartment bulkhead, from within the cockpit,

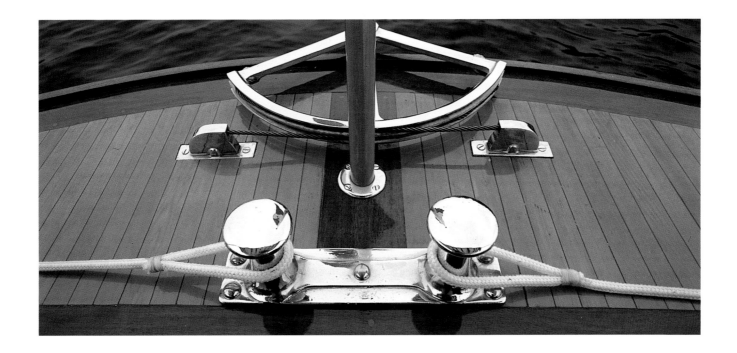

instead of having to climb into the engine compartment to swing a crank.

There were certain drawbacks to building bigger, faster boats. The design became much more critical, and much less forgiving. The

OPPOSITE: Thought to be the oldest Chris-Craft afloat, the **Rainbow IX** *was built as the* **Packard Chriscraft** *in 1922 or 1923 by American builder Chris Smith.*

ABOVE: A rear deck detail of the 1914 Minett-built **Rita**, *a well-loved fixture on the lakes.*

development of a good bottom that resulted in a good-riding boat was as much an art as it was a science in the early days. A bottom could be bought from a naval architect, it could then be reworked, scaled up or down according to what the builder and his customer wanted, and then reworked again if the result did not give satisfaction. Flexibility and individual interpretation were the marks of the master boatbuilder. It isn't clear how many builders in Muskoka bought plans in the early days, or how many simply developed good-riding hulls by trial and error. We do know that in the early 1920s both Ditchburn and Minett built fast, V-bottom boats from plans drawn up by George Crouch.

Dr. John Ross Robertson, a pioneer pilot, is said to have designed for Ditchburn in the teens, but the best-known naval architect associated with Ditchburn was Bert Hawker. Hawker was born in Sittingbourne, Kent, England, in 1885, and at age fourteen he was apprenticed for seven years to his grandfather, Samuel George, who had a shipyard at Sheerness. Hawker came to Canada in about 1906 or 1907 and worked for T.W. Jutten at his boat yard in Hamilton, designing all manner of craft, the largest being a 50-foot cruiser. Five years later he came to Muskoka and went to Minett's works, where, as he put it, "the first deluxe runabouts were built in Canada." Hawker stayed with Minett until 1916, when he joined the Canadian Expeditionary Force and went overseas. Following his demobilization in the spring of 1919, he joined Ditchburn, where he worked until the crash and depression of 1930, when, out of a job, he struck out on his own.

The war years proved a great boom period for boatbuilding in Muskoka. America stayed out of

*Joinery typical of the Muskoka builders: the covering board of the 1935 Minett-Shields **Fancy Lady**.*

the conflict overseas for the first three years, but since its citizens could no longer go to many parts of Europe, a number of them came to Muskoka for their holidays and spent their dollars here, on sensible things such as new boats. The first generation of open launches with cranky two-cycle engines were looking decidedly dated by this time. The newer, long, sleek mahogany motorboat, with its one-man folding top, electric

Launches were equipped with automotive fixtures from the earliest days.

The trend in automobile design, away from open vehicles to bodies with fixed tops, was parallelled by some boatbuilders during the late teens. Ditchburn built a number of launches over 30 feet in length, with permanent, fixed sedan tops. But this became increasingly an oddity in the 1920s, as most launches were equipped with removable navy tops. Ditchburn also started fixing horns, prominently mounted on the forward deck, a practice they maintained until 1930, when they introduced a model with its horn placed below the deck.

Bert Minett advertised in the November 1917 issue of *Canadian Motorboat* that he built "specially refined mahogany models" fitted with electric starter, electric lights, seamless tank, pleated upholstery, aluminum bow stem, special finish and special fittings." He offered several different models: 26 feet long by 5 1/2-foot beam with a 30-horsepower Scripps; 32 feet by 6 feet, with a 65-horsepower Van Blerck; and 35 feet by 7 feet, with a 65-horsepower Van Blerck.

Minett's earlier launches, such as the *Norwood II* (c. 1911) and the *Tango* (1913), were originally equipped with special fittings that

lights and starters, and more powerful engines, was a natural next step for the boating public.

allowed the entire engine hatch, dash and windscreen to be raised up on folding metal supports, or arms, to allow access to the engine compartment. Ditchburn was using hinged hatches by 1914, but Minett didn't offer this feature until 1916.

In September 1918 the *Mineta*, a big new launch, was delivered to Clevelands House from Minett's shop. I have been told that the *Mineta* (the third boat of that name that Bert built) was the first launch built in Muskoka to have a small cockpit with a removable mahogany cover forward of the engine compartment, and that it was among the first Minett launches to have a two-part, hinged, wooden-framed windscreen with side panels. About the same time, Ditchburn was using hinged wooden windscreens that could be swung forward and laid flat on the deck.

The day of the old-style open boat was quickly coming to a close. A new company, the Disappearing Propeller Boat Company, was established in 1916 to manufacture inexpensive, small, and very serviceable boats in Port Carling. These quickly filled the market niche that the older boats had been filling since they had

*ABOVE: The **Mineta** was built as the hotel launch for Clevelands House.*

*OPPOSITE: Bert Minett built the **Mineta** in 1918. The rear deck detail is mesmerizing.*

been displaced from so many launch houses by the new generation of mahogany motorboats. The heyday of the classic custom-built launches of Muskoka was at hand.

THE TWENTIES

T he two great shops active in the 1920s were Ditchburn's and Minett's (from 1925, Minett-Shields). Of the two, Ditchburn was very much the larger concern and by far the more successful. In their two best years Ditchburn built as many boats as Minett-Shields did in their entire existence. Ditchburn cruisers and launches were found in waters from the Maritimes to Vancouver, and south of the border as well. Minett-Shields' boats were much more a local presence; the Muskoka Lakes, Peninsula Lake and Lake of Bays were home waters for pretty well everything that came out of their works.

Ditchburn employed about thirty men in 1920, and by the end of the decade there were about 145 on the payroll. The company had built

*OPPOSITE: The 36-foot Ditchburn displacement launch the **Lady Elgin** was built in 1929 for the Wallace family of Minett and ran as a livery and tour boat for decades.*

one large 73-foot cruiser, the *Kawandag*, in 1916, and a few other day cruisers in the late teens, before building the Bert Hawker-designed 61-foot *Idylese* after the war. This cruiser proved to be the first of a number of truly outstanding large vessels. A new yard was opened in Orillia to build cruisers that were too large to be shipped from Gravenhurst by rail; from Orillia they could be delivered by water via the Trent.

The rough work was done in Orillia, and all the cabinetry and fine finishing work was done in Gravenhurst and shipped down to be fitted. Ditchburn had their own foundry, their own upholstery shop, machinists, blacksmiths, and mechanics. They made the patterns for their hardware. Apart from the engines, they built everything that went into their boats.

But the new cruiser business was just half of the story behind the successes of the company in the 1920s. Harry Greening, one of the greatest and most knowledgeable motorboat racers of his day, established a very good relationship with Ditchburn in 1919 when he had them build the first of six or seven raceboats, the *Rainbows*. Greening's *Rainbows* won a number of races and set many records. He never tired of trying to make his boats go faster than ever before. And they were built by Ditchburn.

As an immediate result of this connection with Greening, Ditchburn started to offer hard-chine launches. Hard-chine means that the bottom was not round, but turned, or had a hard corner where the now distinct sides met the bottom. In simple terms, the bottom was V-shaped forward and gradually flattened until it was flat at the transom, or stern, of the boat.

A round-bottomed boat is more efficient at slower speeds than a V-bottom. In a round-bottomed boat you get more speed for your power, up to a certain point: if the boat has too large an engine, the additional power is wasted trying to climb its own bow wave, and a V-bottom is better. The displacement-type hull will simply settle and, as they say, it "drives hard," where a planing-type hull will rise up and plane, driving more easily.

For 1922 Ditchburn introduced four hard-chine models inspired by the first *Rainbow*: 21 feet by 5 feet 6 inches; 26 feet by 6 feet; 32 feet by 6 feet 6 inches; and 35 feet by 6 feet 6 inches. They had a sharper V-shape and a higher chine line forward than the traditional V-bottom design. Intriguingly, one aspect of these launches' construction that Ditchburn emphasized was the fact that they utilized no sawn or web frames. The frame construction consisted entirely of steam-bent white-oak ribs. The hulls were built of mahogany, with a double-skin bottom.

The standardized round-bottom launches offered by Ditchburn in the early 1920s were 21 feet by 5 feet 6 inches; 26 by 6 feet; 31 feet by 6 feet 6 inches; and 38 feet by 7 feet 6 inches. These Ditchburn round-bottom launches built before 1927 were relatively easy to distinguish from those built from 1927 to 1930 due to the use of a raised engine hatch with a series of vents running down the boat's length in post-1927 models.

Navy tops became increasingly popular in the 1920s, as the so-called one-man top was relegated to the rafters in many launch houses. The one-man top required the efforts of several

*This Minett launch was rebuilt and modernized by Minett-Shields
in the mid-thirties and recently has been unmodernized.*

men of an even disposition to raise and lower the big, old centre-drive launches, while the navy top could be handled by one man. The folding-style convertible top remained popular in the United States because the cockpits of forward-drive runabouts built in the States were much smaller than those built here, and as a result the size of the folding top was much more manageable.

The Disappearing Propeller Boat Company expanded rapidly following the war, and by the early 1920s was the largest manufacturer of motorboats in Canada. Employing about forty hands in their factory in Port Carling, they turned out several hundred Dispros a year for two or three years, until the company ran into financial difficulties in 1924 and was closed down. Before long, a number of its key men started a new concern, the Port Carling Boat Works, above the locks, in competition with a new boatbuilding business established in the

*Disappearing propeller boats such as the **Emily** engender fierce loyalty in their owners.*

old Matheson shop below the locks – Dukes.

The Bracebridge Launch Works disappeared before 1925, but it is not clear whether or not they built any boats in the 1920s. We do know that Minett was on the point of bankruptcy at this time. Bert Minett had moved to a new shop by the river, below the falls in Bracebridge, in about 1923, but within two years his situation had become critical, the wages of his five employees were six months in arrears, and his brother Art, who ran the family hotel, Clevelands House, told Bert that he could no longer afford to keep him in business. One Minett employee, Earl C. Barnes, set out on his own and over the years established a reputation for building boats as well as Bert did. Bert was a perfectionist who was much more concerned with building the finest boat possible than with business. He had a reputation for selling for $6,000 a launch that had cost $7,000 to build.

In the summer of 1925 Minett found a white knight in the person of twenty-five-year-old

Bryson Shields, and the business was reorganized as a private incorporated company with Shields as the president and salesman. Minett could do what he loved — build boats. With adequate capital and Shield's connections (he was related to half a dozen wealthy families on Lake Joseph and knew everyone else who mattered), the new company was in an excellent position to sell expensive custom launches in those boom years at the end of the 1920s.

Minett-Shields was best known in the late 1920s for its big displacement launches. More than a dozen boats from 30 to 36 feet in length were built between 1926 and 1930. With their characteristic Minett lines, they are easily distinguishable from comparable work done at Ditchburn. The stem of a Minett was straighter, and the bow of the hull had noticeably less flare. The line of the deck fell as it approached the stem, an effect that was exaggerated by the continued use of a flush deck — unlike Ditchburn, who adopted a raised engine compartment with ventilators fixed along its length in 1927.

A striking and very effective Minett-Shields innovation was the introduction of a modified-chine aft. In effect, the boats were given a flatter bottom at the transom, holding the bow down and thus permitting more speed than the traditional round-bottomed launch. A 6-inch-by-6-inch piece of cedar, running about one third of the length of the hull, was fitted to the chine and was carved out to fit the ribbed round hull but was squared on the outside. The result was a good-running hull at any speed, one that didn't sacrifice the aesthetic attributes of the traditional design. Ditchburn introduced the same feature in their 31-footers by 1929.

Many thought that Minett went to ridiculous lengths to build what he thought was a good boat. Launches that came from his shop were much more expensive than launches of a comparable size and power sold by Ditchburn; a 34-to-36-foot launch could cost from $12,000 to $13,000 — about a third more than the going price at Ditchburn. A 26-foot hard-chine boat sold for about twenty percent more than a Ditchburn Viking.

Taking a look at the outside, the deck detailing, the hardware, the emphasis on the individuality of each job, helps us understand how Minett-Shields could command this premium, but what went into the construction tells us that much more. Ditchburn built an excellent boat, but Minett went to even greater lengths in his attempt to build the "best" boat.

The standard clauses found in a Minett-Shields contract for a "motor craft, custom built" specified that the transom was to be one piece of mahogany, steam-bent to a circular shape, with an oak strip 4 inches by 1 1/2 inches rabbeted into the bottom edge of the transom; the mahogany and the oak to be bent to the same radius and fitted together cold.

In the displacement launches, ribs were 3/4-by-7/8-inch Erie white oak, steam-bent and fitted full-length, and carefully shimmed with cedar at the keel. They were spaced on 6-inch centres. The fore-end ribs, at the flare, were bent on templates and also fitted cold. The ribs carrying the engine foundation were larger, 3/4 inch by 1 3/4 inches, as were ribs installed at places where excessive stress could be expected, near the rudder, at the strut and at the shaft log. Hard-chine boats were made slightly stronger: ribs were 1/2 inch by 5/8 inch spaced on 3-inch centres on the bottom and 6-inch on the sides.

Deck frames were made of clear spruce, sawn to shape "according to our usual practice," spaced on 10-inch centres. In at least some cases, Ditchburn used steam-bent frames that could flatten over time.

The standard contract from the mid-twenties specified that galvanized screws were to be used, so presumably it had been common practice to use steel screws by that time. From 1928 brass screws were generally specified.

Minett stated that the mahogany planking would be finished to 9/16 inches, that the planks would be spiled to shape and hollowed to fit the form of the boat, and that they would not be dished by steam or water. The bottoms were planked with clear Ontario cedar, fitted, then given two coats of varnish before being fixed in place.

One of the more intriguing details about these old boats is the finish of the hardware or deck fittings. Polished brass was standard in the early days, Ditchburn was using highly polished aluminum in the teens, and like Minett, he started using nickel-plated brass and bronze before 1920.

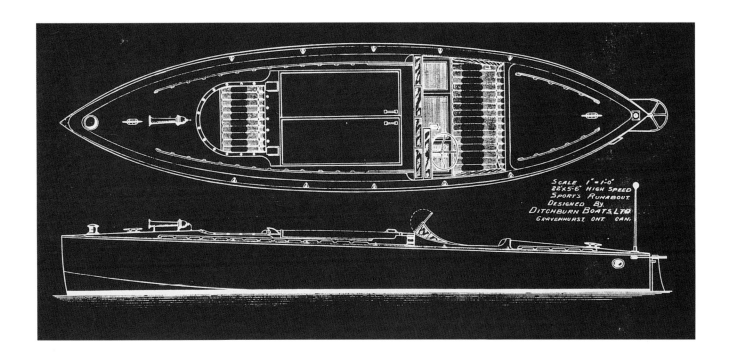

Plans for a Ditchburn 22-footer, built for speed.

Down in the States, in the mid to late twenties, Chris-Craft was using white metal; Gar Wood, Monel metal (67 percent nickel, 28 percent copper); Hacker, German silver; and Dodge, brass.

The Ford Motor Company changed the trim on their line of automobiles to chromium plate in 1927, and those automobile manufacturers who were not using chromium plate soon followed the industry leader. Not surprisingly, given the dependence of boat manufacturers on the automobile parts suppliers and the tremendous influence that changes in automobile design and styling had on the expectations of the boat-buying public, the boatbuilders followed. Minett-Shields started using chromium plate in 1928, Ditchburn in 1930, and all the major American builders changed over between 1930 and 1931.

One of the most difficult questions that arises when examining an old launch concerns the instrumentation. Most of the older launches have been fitted out with new, more dependable

The **Flip-a-coin** is a 27-foot Ditchburn Viking equipped with the
streamlined 1930 Ditchburn hardware.

used until 1928 or 1929 in some of the larger models. The forward navigation light is a very streamlined mahogany fixture, much more typical of the early 1930s than of anything else that was seen on these lakes.

Ditchburn, Minett-Shields, Barnes, and Greavette all designed and cast most of their own deck hardware; many of the other Muskoka boatbuilders bought stock hardware from firms such as Foreman or Leckies; and Ditchburn sold some of their fittings to the independents, as well. The bigger Dukes built in the early 1930s all have 1930-pattern Ditchburn hardware.

The clamshell- or half-bell-shaped engine ventilator was in use in the United States by 1924 and was used from 1927 or 1928 by Minett-Shields. In 1928 Minett-Shields started fitting "Half-mile Ray" spotlights to the central windscreen strut; this became common in 1929. The more streamlined swept-back forward navigation light with built-in vents set on either side was being used by Hacker in 1927 and was again adopted by Minett-Shields for their bigger boats in 1928 and 1929; before that time they used a round nickel-plated fixture.

Minett-Shields were the first to popularize the painting of launch bottoms bronze or copper, around 1926 or 1927. Bottoms from all builders traditionally had been painted green or red. The late Aub Bud of Milford Bay speculated that ninety percent of the boats on these waters had green-painted bottoms up to that time. To keep the bottoms presentable they had to be stripped and repainted periodically: the advantage of the copper-bronze paints lay in the fact that the paint would gradually wear away and a new coat could be applied much more easily. Even though the paint had been developed as a special anti-fouling surface — which was not, of course, a problem in fresh water — it looked very smart contrasting with the deeply stained, highly finished mahogany hull. However, it must be noted that, with custom work, the underbodies were painted any colour the contracting purchaser ordered. *Norwood II*, for instance, always had a varnished bottom, and Craigs' *Wacoutta II* was painted a flat black.

By the late 1920s most of the boats built in Muskoka were several years out of date, compared to the work being done south of

Minett ventilator patterns from the mid-thirties.

the border. By 1924 the major American builders offered only hard-chine runabouts; the displacement-type hull for smaller launches had been abandoned in favour of the V-bottom. In 1918 John L. Hacker had designed the Belle Island Bear Cats, a line of V-bottomed forward-drive launches, for Belle Island. (I'm sure the use of a name that would make a purchaser think of the Stutz Bearcat was unintentional.) The Bear Cat's general configuration was subsequently adopted by Chris-Craft, Gar Wood and Dodge

when they embarked on large-scale production in the early 1920s. On the other hand, Duke's in Port Carling built a very handsome round-bottom launch into the 1960s, using building techniques that Charlie Duke had learned as a boatbuilder at Ditchburn's works in the teens.

Looking at publicity photos of American-built Dart boats from 1928, you can't help but be impressed how different, and how much more modern, they appeared from what was being built in Muskoka. The Dart was a hard-chine launch, with batten-seam construction, forward drive, two cockpits forward and one aft, and compared to the pronounced tumblehome of the typical Muskoka-built launch, a rather square stern. But closer inspection reveals that even the utilities in Muskoka were trimmed to a much higher standard. The Dart boats look cheaply knocked-off if compared side by side with even an inexpensive, old-fashioned SeaBirD from the same era. With their two-toned decks, wide and forgiving deck planking, lack of edging trim for the deck planks to butt into, no windscreen, dome-fastened canvas cover for the aft cockpit, and no coaming, the Darts look mass-produced — and they were. But they sold by the hundreds, and they made money.

While 1928 proved a great year for all the Muskoka shops, 1929 proved even better. Two Ditchburn employees, David Fettes and William Hall, struck out on their own and built a prototype for a standardized forward-drive, 18-foot, step-hulled, fast, yet moderately priced, boat for Ellsworth Flavelle. They formed a partnership and in the spring of 1930 arranged for William Ogilvie to represent them in Toronto.

In Port Carling, William Johnston Jr. left the Port Carling Boat Works and opened his own shop in the old Disappearing Propeller Boat factory. The boatworks continued to grow, and over the years established a niche as a builder of good-running, serviceable small launches called SeaBirDs, 20- and 23-footers of both clinker and smoothskin, or carvel, construction.

Hans Sachau opened a yard in Toronto on the Humber River in the late 1920s; J.J. Taylor expanded and developed a line of stock cruisers; and Bert Duke and Bill Ogilvie opened a new business building stock "Sea Swift" launches in Toronto. A new factory was built by Janney-Gilbert in Kingston to build both standardized boats and aircraft in 1928. The market for new launches and faster V-bottomed boats seemed insatiable.

The constant growth in the demand for runabouts in the United States sparked a huge expansion: Dodge and Gar Wood built new large factories; and Chris-Craft expanded their works at Algonac yet again, as they turned out ever-increasing numbers of standardized runabouts of both longer and shorter lengths than ever before. Gar Wood and Chris-Craft advertised widely in Canada, and while they had not yet made their mark in Muskoka, they had certainly established a solid presence elsewhere in the country.

THE THIRTIES

T he stock market crash in the fall of 1929 put a tragically spectacular end to the boom years of the late 1920s. Of course, business did not come to a complete halt immediately; the economy started to shrink in the winter of 1929, and then kept on shrinking for the next two or three years. No one had any idea that first winter just how severe this depression would be.

In expectation of a speedy economic recovery and the resumption of market expansion like that experienced in 1928 and 1929, the various boatbuilders proceeded with their plans for the new season. And in 1930 there was a great deal of change in the industry in Muskoka. After years of growth in sales, and with its close association with the high-profile members of the racing community and a reputation as the preeminent builder of custom cruisers in Canada, Ditchburn

*Opposite: Delivered in 1928, the **Wascana II** has since been fitted with a navy top, splash rails, and a number of ventilators.*

entered the new decade poised for even greater things. Tens of thousands of dollars were invested in new plant and equipment in Gravenhurst. New designs for established lines were under way, prototypes for new models were being built, and interesting experimental work was being carried out on the development of an external stern drive for launches.

In addition to the expansion of the Gravenhurst works in late 1929, plans were made to market their launches and cruisers more aggressively. In January 1930 Ditchburn Marine Sales Ltd. opened a showroom on King Street in Toronto, where they carried Ditchburn boats, of course, but also showed models offered by Port Carling Boatworks, the Disappearing Propeller Boat Company, and the Peterborough Canoe Company. They were also Ontario distributors for Sterling marine engines, Buchanan Bulldog engines, and Winton diesels. In addition, they sold Evinrude and Johnson outboard motors, and

Van Blerck inboard engines. Rope fenders made by the Newark Rope Works and Tom Taylor were also stocked.

Ditchburn changed the look of their stock hard-chine, or V-bottom, launches dramatically for the new season. The Viking was changed to forward-drive and took on an appearance that was much more American. A flat windscreen with an upswept forward deck and a raised coaming that ran the length of the two cockpits and engine compartment characterized the new design. A new, smaller V-bottomed model, 24 feet by 6 feet, called the Neptune, was introduced, and the deck hardware was redesigned for all models. This new pattern was decidedly more streamlined than the old. But the older style of motorboat was not thrown over completely. Two stock models of round-bilge launches were still advertised: the 31-foot Commodore and the 26-foot Roamer. A new, smaller boat was introduced. This very attractive, fast, shingled-bottomed "speedster" was built for the Wardwells. It was the prototype for a series that was called the Rainbow Junior, but it would appear that only about three of these were ever built. The

only one that I know of that has survived is the Formans' *L'Aiglon*.

This optimism for the new season wasn't limited to Ditchburn. Fetthall was reportedly working two shifts in the spring of 1930. They had introduced an 18-foot mahogany hydroplane powered by a 25-horsepower Van Blerck with a stern drive. This was offered for $1,295 F.O.B. Gravenhurst, taxes extra.

In Bracebridge, Minett-Shields finished two large cruisers in 1930 and built two or three 30-foot hard-chine launches. These boats featured a number of striking changes in both styling and construction. Cast-aluminum transom frames were used for the first time; the forward navigation light was set into the stem, immediately below the deck line; and the port and starboard navigation lights were placed in compartments recessed into the hull. The general layout was similar on all of these launches, with two cockpits forward and one aft. The *Scudd II*, ordered by the Pecks on Lake of Bays, was probably the first of these built.

The company ran a number of advertisements in the quality press in an attempt to present

*The **Eaglet II**.*

themselves as not only the premium builders of custom motorboats, but of cruisers, as well. New orders started to dry up, however, and it is said that all outstanding contracts were cancelled in the summer of 1930. Everyone was laid off.

Earl Barnes was making a name for himself, and in addition to advertising regularly in the press, he too engaged William Ogilvie to represent his shop in Toronto in the fall of 1930. But he soon ran into difficulties with cancelled

orders and was left struggling to sell finished boats at sacrifice prices. The other Bracebridge builder, Clive Brown, was trading under the name Brown Boat and Motor Works in 1930. He offered an attractive 20-foot-by-5-foot-3-inch, hard-chine, forward-drive boat powered by a custom-built Brown engine, all for $1,850.

But the real news that year was in Gravenhurst. In August 1930 Tom Greavette's resignation from Ditchburn was announced in the press, and at the same time rumours were published that a new company, Rainbow Craft, was in the process of being established to build what was referred to as "standardized" boats. This was devastating news for Ditchburn. Tom Greavette had been with Ditchburn since he was a boy. He had built rowboats in Gravenhurst in the 1890s, had been made a director when Ditchburn was incorporated in 1907, and had been in charge of sales for years. In the boating press he was described as the man who had sold more boats worth more than $500 than any other man in Canada.

Small-boat orders at Ditchburn had evaporated in the summer of 1930, and with no work on the books for the coming winter, the news of a key

The New 1930 Ditchburn Models

Justify Great Expectations

Ditchburn goes for the American look.

man leaving and a new competitor entering an already overcrowded market was the last thing that the company needed.

In a short time Greavette's decision to jump ship, so to speak, was followed by the news of his taking a position with Rainbow Craft. Herbert Ditchburn was incensed and demanded that the new company change its name, which it did. It started business as Greavette Boats Limited. Rainbow Craft had advertised that they would commence production on January 2, 1931. In November 1930 advertisements appeared in *Canadian Power Boating* headlined, "The Coming of the Rainbow." The ads described the new company's plans to mass-produce a few stock models, imitating the successful methods

of such big American factories as Chris-Craft and Dodge.

On December 24, 1930, two prototype models, a 24-footer and a 19-footer, were shipped to Toronto and tried out in the bay. The trials didn't start until the late afternoon, as a channel had to be cut through the ice to open water. Full production started that spring, with most of the key men who had worked for Ditchburn for years on the new company's payroll.

Boats had never been built in Muskoka like they were built at Greavette. A "time and

Is it a Dart? Is it a Chris-Craft? No, it's just an American-style Greavette.

efficiency" expert from General Motors came up and helped develop a production line that allowed for the building an 18-footer in eleven and a half hours. Greavette offered four stock models: the 18-foot Ensign, the 18-foot Roamer, the 23-foot Mohawk, and the 26-foot Comet. They looked like any one of the stock American boats of the day: hard-chine, double-skin bottom, chrome cutwater, and all bottoms painted copper. They

Ditchburn-built launches were fitted with small brass plates.

rode well and were quite serviceable, but they were nothing exciting to look at. Oscar Purdy recalls, they were "a dime-a-dozen boat."

A Toronto salesroom was opened on March 1, 1931, at 121 King Street West, and advertisements were published inviting prospective dealers to take up territories across the country. The new works went into full production in April 1931, and for the next eighteen months operated sporadically, shutting down periodically to clear unsold inventory and collect enough orders to warrant reopening the shop. By the end of 1932 it was clear that there was no future for the company if it was to continue building stock launches on a large production basis. In the winter of 1932–33 the company was reorganized, its officers were changed, and most importantly, an exclusive arrangement with famous naval architect John L. Hacker was announced. A new commitment to custom boatbuilding was published in the papers.

Greavette's line of stock launches was dropped in 1933, and Hacker drew up plans for three new boats — the 26-foot Commander, the 23-foot Dictator, and the 19-foot Special — that were to be built to order. That same year, at least two new custom 33-footers were also built. The new stock launches were quite different in appearance from the dated Dart designs that had been employed to that time. The decks were now flush, the tumblehome more pronounced, and a more streamlined look adopted.

John Hacker was well known in Canadian boating circles. He had been advertising in the Canadian trade magazines for years and had sold plans to many of the different builders. He had developed a particularly close working relationship with a builder in Quebec's Eastern Townships: the Woodard-McCrea Boatworks in North Hatley, Quebec, stated in their logo that their boats were all Hacker-designed. Ditchburn had used Hacker's plans, and Minett-Shields had bought at least three hard-chine bottoms from him between 1927 and 1933.

The full effects of the Depression began to hit hard in the summer of 1930. In November Ditchburn got an order for a large cruiser. The order would result in two hundred ten-hour days for fifteen men, but the job was too big for Gravenhurst, so it was decided that the cruiser would be built in Orillia. There was nothing on the books in Gravenhurst, and everyone was laid off.

After a decade of large annual increases in both the number and value of boats built in Muskoka, the demand for cruisers and large custom launches collapsed in 1930. Ditchburn struggled on in 1931, and while it produced forty percent of the value of the entire industry in Canada, it was forty percent of an industry that had shrunk by almost two thirds in one short year. Herb Ditchburn predicted further shrinkage for 1932 and thought that the entire output of all builders in Canada would amount to only about fifteen percent of the business that had been done in 1929–1930.

In 1930 it was estimated that a 50-foot cruiser could be bought for about $50,000; a high-speed runabout for about $6,000; and a moderate-sized launch, 18 to 25 feet, with an engine of about 30 horsepower, for about $1,500.

In January 1931 *Canadian Power Boating* published the results of an industry survey that included a forecast of the market for the coming year. The article suggested that no fewer than ten 40-mile-per-hour-and-over launches would be required (at about $6,000 each); a hundred 20-mile-per-hour boats at $ 2,000 each; and 400 inboard knockabouts at about $1,000 each. It also noted that the United States "invasion" of motor craft had just begun; in 1930, 120 motorboats had been imported. Gar Wood and Chris-Craft advertised extensively in Canadian publications from the late 1920s but don't appear to have had Canadian agents at that time. Hudson-Essex York of Toronto were appointed Ontario representatives for Dodge Boats in the spring of 1931, and Evan Fraling was representing Chris-Craft in Muskoka by the late 1930s.

In the February 1931 issue of *Canadian Power Boating* a standardized boat buyers' guide was printed that gives us a picture of what the domestic industry was offering in the Canadian market. Barnes advertised three models, from 22 1/2 feet to 30 feet in length, all Chrysler powered. Port Carling had two models, 20 feet and 23 feet, powered by Buchanan. Ditchburn listed eight different runabouts, from 21 feet to 34 feet, and three cruisers, 26 feet to 38 feet. Fetthall offered three runabouts, 17 feet to 21 feet, with Falcon engines. Johnston had an 18-footer and a 21-foot model, powered by Chrysler and Falcon. Johnston also built a line of 15-foot and 17-foot outboards.

While these boats were offered, not many were purchased. Fetthall folded at the end of the year, and the two principals went to work for a new shop, the Scott Boatworks in Toronto, which built cheaper boats. Minett-Shields was closed up

A Minett-Shields advertisement from December 1931, a time when the company was in trouble.

more often than not in the early thirties. Only five new boats were built from 1930 to the fall of 1933. Burdened by high debt incurred in the big expansion of 1929, Ditchburn hiccuped and wheezed, surviving hand to mouth as the odd order came through. Greavette looked like it was going to prove to be a flash in the pan, but well capitalized, with a group of solid backers, it kept on.

Curiously, some of the small shops were better positioned to weather the financial storm than the high fliers. As my great-grandfather (a Scot) used to say, "The higher you fly, the further you fall." Ditchburn flew high and, encumbered with a large, unserviceable debt, fell fast. Tied so closely to the top of the market, Minett-Shields had nothing to fall back on when that market evaporated. Earl Barnes built a few launches each year in his small shop, and while he certainly never made a fortune, he carried on building the smaller launches that Minett-Shields had once built, at a modest price.

In Port Carling, the Port Carling Boatworks, ably managed and perfectly positioned in the market, with small, serviceable, tight watercraft, met the equally tight pockets of a much less particular buying public. Their boats were no longer just the second boat in many families, but had become the primary craft.

Just downstream, on the other side of the locks, Duke's was busy building the first of what

was to prove a very successful model, the 18-foot lapstrake Playmate.

In the spring of 1933 the economy began to turn for the better, or at least it stopped its relentless descent. Ditchburn was reorganized as the Ditchburn Boat and Yachting Co. Ltd. and went back into business — a much changed business — offering smaller utility-type boats, as well as bidding for the larger cruiser order that still came along. Greavette's was reorganized and started to build some really interesting custom boats. It also began building the first of what would become a string of racing boats for Harold Wilson.

Minett-Shields had reopened and built a few custom launches in 1933. The *Queen*, a V-bottom 26-footer built for Allan Neilson, has the same hull as the Hacker-inspired bottoms first built in 1927, but the hardware that was installed on her is an interesting mixture of both late twenties and early thirties styles. The forward cockpit was equipped with the two-part double-curved plate-glass screens that evolved from the first single-sheet double-curved screen built by W.L. Claus for his *Norwood III* in 1926

The Playmate became the most popular launch Duke built.

and subsequently used on a number of other boats built in the late twenties; the rear two cockpits featured the basic two flat-plate screens mounted on an angle that was the standard into the 1950s.

The old clamshell, or half-bell, chrome ventilators introduced by 1928 were abandoned in favour of the more streamlined chrome teardrop of the same general size as the old ventilator in 1933. The following year Minett-Shields introduced some striking innovations in the trimming of their launches with streamlined carved-mahogany ventilators and navigation lights inset into the hull. Ditchburn and Greavette adopted a chrome-trimmed inset navigation light shortly thereafter.

In 1934 Minett-Shields built for F.C. Burgess what is to my eye an extraordinarily pleasing 24-foot V-bottom launch highlighting these new features and also getting a jump on the competition by streamlining the hull and pulling in the tumblehome in an even more dramatic fashion than they had with the Hamlins' *Hoo Doo* seven years earlier. This boat unfortunately burned at the end of its first season when a gas line broke and the bilge filled with gas, with predictable results. But from a series of photos taken during the boat's trials, it is clear that a lightness and grace was exemplified that did not show up in the massive bulk of the streamliners built by Greavette a number of years later. Then again, they were building in an era when the aesthetics of what was considered good design were changing to a distinctly larger-than-life look — think of what was happening to automobiles!

The same year that Minett-Shields was building this 24-footer for Burgess, they started building a very popular 18-foot Class E, or sports, runabout. This highly successful rear-drive boat was the smallest launch to have come out of the works. The same bottom was lengthened to 21 feet and the controls moved up to the forward station; both cockpits were protected with two-piece angled windscreens, the forward cockpit's screen with the standard half-mile ray spotlight mounted on the central strut. Both models were built with inset navigation lights (first used in 1930 and 1931 on 30-footers such as the *Glen Avy II* and the *Scud II*). The streamlined, long teardrop mahogany ventilators and the new windswept cast hardware with the distinctive fishtail exhaust pipes enhanced an already modern styling.

Again in 1934, they made another switch and offered to paint their bottoms a cream or buff colour, generally with no contrasting boot top. This colour dramatically emphasized the crisp line of the chine as it rose from the spray thrown aft to meld into the flat plane of the hull forward. It worked especially well in these waters because of the lakes' clarity; obviously the effect would have been lost if the waters were dirty and the bottoms were not pristine.

The American Power Boat Association authorized a new class of racing boats in 1934, the 225. The rules governing the 225 class provide that the boats had to have a waterline length of not less than 15 1/2 feet; a waterline beam width, at their widest section, of no less than 4 1/2 feet; seat two persons (and carry a crew of two in all races); and the total displacement of the motors was not to exceed 225 cubic inches. The retail price of the complete motor was not to exceed $700. It quickly became a very popular class of racing boat, and one of the first international regattas featuring the 225s was held that season in Toronto.

A series of three races was run at the Canadian National Exhibition in August 1934. Practically all the 225-class hydroplanes in commission in the United States and Canada made a showing. Among the entrants were two Greavette-built boats and two Ditchburns. This was to prove an auspicious debut in a class that was to retain great popularity for the rest of the decade.

P.J. Campbell bought a 225-class Ventnor-designed speedboat from the J.C. Scott works in Toronto. Based on Lake Scugog, *Marguerite IV* was powered by a Kermath V-8 and in 1935 was considered to be the fastest of her class in Canada. Impressed by her showing in Canada and the consistent winning records of the Arnold Apel-designed Ventnor Craft stock hulls in the United States, Bryson Shields made arrangements to build the Apel-designed hulls under licence in Canada in February or March 1936. Over the next two or three years, he built at least half a dozen, many for the same young men who had purchased his 18-foot Class-E

A young man's fancy turns to — an 18-foot Greavette Flash.

sport racers a couple of years before, but who were now interested in graduating to something with a lot more power.

At the National Automotive Show held in Toronto in January 1935, there was a section devoted to boats, with two cruisers, twelve runabouts and three outboards exhibited by Barnes, Scott, Port Carling Boat Works, Greavette, and Grew. It was noted in the press that the Canadian builders, unlike the Americans, were moving away from the V-bottom in favour of a rounder bottom to give a softer ride. These were not the old round-bottomed displacement-type hulls of the 1920s, but rather than a hard break at the chine, there was a curvature that increased in sharpness toward the stern, where the bottom was nearly flat. Greavette

*The **Delta**, built by Minett-Shields in 1936. The next step for the speed demons.*

called this their "non-pounding hull," and Barnes sold it as his "cushioned bottom."

Boatbuilding in Port Carling thrived from the mid-1930s. Duke's had built a number of custom launches up to 30 feet in length in the late 1920s, but their mainstay from 1934 was the Playmate, an 18-foot lapstrake utility boat. The Port Carling Boat Works was building more boats than anyone else on the lakes by the end of the decade, up to fifty a year were coming out of their shop, and before the war there were probably more SeaBirDs in use on the lakes than any other make of boat.

While I have no shop records for any of the firms, it would appear likely that over the winter of 1935–36 there were about sixty boats built in Gravenhurst, about a dozen in Bracebridge, and perhaps another sixty in Port Carling —

significantly more than had been built in golden days of the late 1920s. But these were smaller boats, priced much more competitively than those built in the earlier, palmy days. And given that the orders were split between so many more shops, the situation was actually worse. Barnes folded, Ditchburn was on the ropes once again, and it isn't at all clear how Minett-Shields managed to hang on — unless of course Uncle Alec (R.A. Shields) was still the proverbial white knight for boatbuilders in distress.

In 1935 Fred Burgess ordered a custom motorboat from Greavette that must rank among the finest big, forward-drive launches ever built in Muskoka. The *Curlew* was designed by John L. Hacker, who was responsible for all the Greavette designs. Hacker made several trips to Gravenhurst to supervise her construction. Because the streamlined curves of the covering board and torpedo stern were something totally new for the workmen at Greavette, he brought George Tanner, an expert builder from the States, to teach Len Barnes how to build a rounded sheer, where the hull melded with the deck line without a break.

That same winter three somewhat similar 26-footers were built by Minett-Shields; Harold Balm's *Caprice II* is the only launch of this design known to survive. Also in Bracebridge, Earl Barnes was building at least one launch, 23 feet by 6 feet 4 inches, that tried to capture the same spirit, for a client who summered on Lake Temagami.

Ditchburn failed again and was reorganized in early 1936, now trading under the name Ditchburn Boats & Aircraft (1936) Ltd. The company embarked on an extensive advertising campaign to re-establish themselves in their traditional market, custom-built large cruisers, and in addition offered an extensive line of boats ranging from a stock 26-foot cruiser to launches from 17 feet to 30 feet.

Their bestselling boat was a 20-footer that came in two models, both flush-decked, two cockpits forward and one aft of the engine, with recessed chrome-trimmed teardrop-shaped navigation lights. The only significant difference lay in the more pronounced tumblehome and a slightly more exaggerated hogged shearline aft on the more streamlined model, which

SETTING THE STANDARD

Lightning, Norwood II, Norwood III, Tango, Ardmore, Shirl-Evon,Gudabi

It is very difficult for us today to appreciate just how quickly motorboating evolved within its first twenty-five years. The first launch was brought up to these waters in 1896; Muskoka boatbuilders first turned to building gasoline launches in about 1903; and some eight or nine years later Bert Minett launched *Norwood II.*

The first generation of motorboats had a distinct look. Close to the water, built with graceful, flowing lines, these old open boats numbered in the hundreds by 1914. They were almost always painted white and were powered with an astounding array of small engines, with distinctly varying degrees of success. The *Floss* is a fine example of one of these early launches.

*OPPOSITE: A 32-foot Minett, the **Tango** was delivered in 1914. She underwent some remodelling about 1930, but her hull is unchanged.*

The *Lightning*, while not original, has a unique history of its own. The engine is said to have been the first four-cycle engine seen on the lakes. It came out of an American-built Elco that had been brought to Muskoka by the Eatons in about 1905. The late Cameron Peck, who assembled a marvellous collection of boats and engines on Lake of Bays in the 1930s and 1940s, purchased the engine, and in 1948 had Bert Hawker design, and Greavette build, a racing boat typical of the period. Hawker had been building and designing boats in the early 1900s and knew what he was up to. The *Lightning* was the result.

Within a very few years there was a complete change in Muskoka's launches. More efficient engines, more power coupled with greater dependability, resulted in the building of larger, longer boats, boats that were increasingly influenced more by automobile design than by the conventions that had traditionally governed the appearance of small boats.

These new, more powerful engines were much more expensive than the old bangers, and the new launches that they were installed in reflected the increased investment, incorporating more imported mahogany, custom-cast deck hardware, automobile-type controls and windshields. By the late teens launches were being built with hard sedan tops that looked as if they were simply landau-type touring cars grafted onto a mahogany hull.

Canadian Motor Boat described a new Minett launch in 1917 that was built for the Clemsons on Lake Muskoka:

"Crashing against a head wind with the solid green curling high, and breaking even with the gunwale, yet rolling in the V-shape and closing up the furrow as if nothing but the wind disturbed the surface, *Spero III*, presents a most spectacular appearance.

"She is 38 by 6 feet, one of those long roomy runabouts that displace a lot of water yet have lines so fine that they slip along with very little disturbance and with such a smooth acceleration that, excepting for the passing shoreline, one has no idea how fast the craft is travelling."

Norwood II numbers among the earliest of these early displacement launches that is still on the lakes. Built for speed, it is as long and as narrow as one would think a boat could be without endangering all aboard! *Norwood III* was built by Minett-Shields for the same family fourteen or fifteen years later and, while clearly embodying the same spirit as her older sister, reflects a number of developments in detailing, and in a many ways anticipated the more streamlined features that were to become standard in all the shops ten years later.

OPPOSITE LEFT: *The **Lightning** was built around this four-cycle engine, reputedly the first on these waters.*

OPPOSITE RIGHT: *The rhythmic pattern of contrasting deck seams makes a pretty picture.*

Spoon bow and beaver-tail stern. Windscreens were first installed

on launches in about 1908.

*Built by Bert Minett and probably delivered in 1911, **Norwood II***

was one of the fastest launches on the lakes.

*Opposite and this page: The **Norwood II** was taken back to the works in 1926 and her engine moved to her new sister, **Norwood III**, then under construction. At the same time, the engine hatches were rebuilt so that they were hinged, and the old cowl ventilator was removed for a more modern fitting. Otherwise, she still looks exactly as she did before the First World War. The view looking dead astern when she is at speed captures the marvellous wings of water that bracket the old displacement speedboats.*

Sisters **Norwood II** and **Norwood III**. Both launches remain in the hands of descendants of the original owner. Built about fourteen years apart, they are different interpretations of the same ideal. **Norwood III** (seen in the background ABOVE and in both views OPPOSITE) is a little beamier, and with her curved plate-glass windscreen (among the first manufactured), streamlined navigation lights, and gently rounded covering board, she stands alone in the fleet.

A Minett (left) and Ditchburn (right) in classic silhouette.

ABOVE AND RIGHT: The **Tango** was originally painted white with a green bottom. Powered by a six-cylinder Van Blerck, she could outrun the **Norwood II**. In 1930 she was turned in on a new Minett-Shields 34-footer — the launch pictured in the advertisement on page 54. The engine ventilators and spotlight date from her refitting at that time.

*OPPOSITE, ABOVE AND RIGHT: The **Ardmore** is a 26-foot Minett built in about 1916, four years after the **Tango**. Engine hatches were now hinged, rather than raised as a single unit on folding brackets. The tubular metal automobile windscreen has been replaced by a two-part wooden-framed assembly that can be dropped forward from a central strut and fixed to the deck.*

*Opposite left: The **Ardmore**.*

*Above and opposite right: The 34-foot Ditchburn-built **Gudahi**, a contemporary of the **Ardmore**, dates from 1916. Note that the deck is slightly recessed below the covering board. This was a Ditchburn practice for many years.*

*OPPOSITE LEFT AND OPPOSITE ABOVE RIGHT: The **Gudahi** is fitted with a specially designed wooden-framed windscreen that, like the older tubular metal auto patterns, could be lowered to the deck in front of the driver. This was apparently only used for one or two years before the adoption of the removable two-part windscreen seen above on the **Shirl-Evon**, a 38-foot Ditchburn built in 1921.*

MAKING A STATEMENT

ROBINBROOK, BLYTHEWOOD II, WIGGIE III, NANIWA II, MARMILWOOD, MARCO, SEA HORSE, EAGLET II

Big displacement launches, boats over 28 feet in length, were being built in Muskoka by 1911. The then heavy power-to-weight factor of the early marine engines, coupled with the very narrow beams of these early boats, necessitated a proportional increase in length to allow for the installation of motors capable of the speeds that were demanded by the boating public. Muskoka boat buyers wanted a launch that would carry more than six people at a reasonable speed and in relative comfort. Given the technology of the day, this demanded a launch of 30 feet or more. In displacement boats, speed is governed by the length.

Most of the earlier launches were built of cedar or cypress and painted white, with varnished mahogany decks and trim, but before the First World War it became increasingly common on the bigger boats to use cedar planking on the bottoms and only mahogany above water. By 1920 a painted hull on anything but a smaller, less expensive launch was distinctly old-fashioned.

But given these parameters, the different shops produced strikingly different launches. Ditchburn was, of course, the most successful, and built dozens of large craft from 30 to 38 feet in length that were, by Canadian standards, "standardized" launches. Minett, whose true love was these long, round-bottomed launches, used his bottom and reworked the topsides repeatedly in producing "individuals." He was building 34-foot displacement vessels into the 1930s that resembled, in many ways, what he had been building twenty years earlier.

*OPPOSITE: The **Sea Horse**, a 34-foot Minett-Shields delivered in 1928.*

It must be remembered that builders like Gidley on Georgian Bay and Mac-Nor at Bala, as well as other minor builders in Muskoka, were building a similar if somewhat less refined craft at the same time. Many men in Muskoka, especially those who worked on the lakes in the summer but who had no winter employment, would build a launch over the winter to keep body and soul together.

The *Robinbrook* is a good example of a big Ditchburn from the twenties. It has the fine riding characteristics of the work that came from the Ditchburn shop in Gravenhurst and exhibits the detailing that exemplified the launches that came out of their shop from about 1920 to 1927.

The Minett and Minett-Shields launches stand more as individuals in their own right than do comparable boats from Ditchburn. It is not that their bottoms changed to any appreciable degree – the only difference that Minett offered from the mid-1920s was the modified-chine aft as described in the introduction – but the topsides, the internal seating, and the detailing of the decking and hardware was to a more pronounced

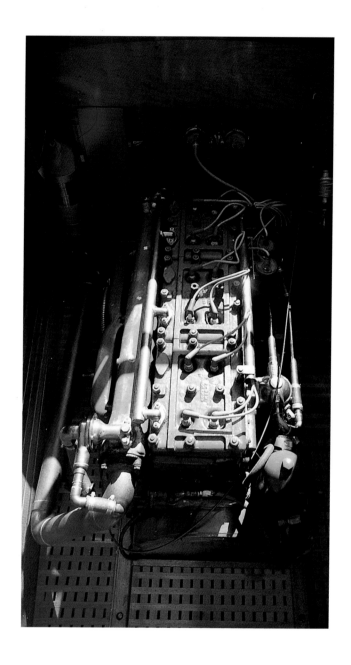

degree a custom agreement between the contracting buyer and the builder.

The **Robinbrook**, a 36-foot Ditchburn dating from 1926. Powered by a Sterling (OPPOSITE), she handles surprisingly well given her imposing bulk. The spotlight is almost certainly a later addition, and the current dark colour of her finish is much more in keeping with Minett's practice than Ditchburn's.

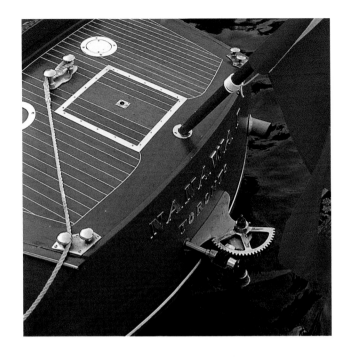

*Opposite: The differences between a Ditchburn, the **Robinbrook**, and a Minett-Shields, the **Naniwa**, can be seen here — the Minett's straighter stem, the angle of the stern flagpole, the drop of the bow deck as it approaches the stem, and the distinctive windscreen.*

*Above: **Naniwa**'s fancy nameplate was given to the family by a friend in the late fifties. Too bad about the spelling!*

*Above right: **Naniwa II**'s outboard rudder.*

*Below: The **Marco** with cast transom frames.*

*Opposite, above and right: The **Blythewood II** is an outstanding example of a Ditchburn day cruiser. Launches with fixed sedan tops were not at all unusual in the teens, but I have only heard of four or five that were built in the twenties. Constructed of vermilion wood, she was notoriously hard to put together and finish. Sixty years later, the men who worked on her new, remembered her and shuddered.*

Opposite, above and right: The **Wiggie III**, *a 1924 31-foot Ditchburn, is a good example of an early 1920s launch, with her flush decks, all-metal hardware, and a horn prominently mounted on her forward deck. Note how the boot top, or waterline, and bottom paint covers the stem. This was usually left unpainted on Minett-Shields boats.*

*OPPOSITE ABOVE: The **Marmilwood** is generally considered the first launch to have been restored (in 1966), as compared to being repaired. A 1927 Minett, she has been fitted with cowl ventilators from an earlier era and a spotlight from a later period. The detail of the lamp ornament (OPPOSITE BELOW LEFT) is found on the Sea Horse. The Minett "keyhole" deck detail (OPPOSITE BELOW RIGHT) is typical of the bigger launches.*

*ABOVE: The **Eaglet II** is one of the more spectacular big launches on the lakes. The dash (BELOW RIGHT) is original and the silver-plate plaque is representative of those mounted by Minett-Shields on their custom work from 1926.*

THE FAMILY LAUNCH

DUQUESNE, WIMUR, SILVERWINGS II, WASCANA II, ALGOMA

The traditional 26-foot mahogany displacement launch was the most popular size of boat built until the early 1930s. By the mid-twenties it had been increased in girth and was generally built with a 6- or even 6 1/2-foot beam, rather than the 5- or 5 1/2-foot beam that had been standard prior to this period.

Anything shorter was more of a utility. Ditchburn built a number of 23-foot and 24-foot displacement boats in the twenties, often of cedar or cypress – what Lionel Cope refers to as chauffeurs' boats. Minett built a few launches about 20 feet in length in the teens and early 1920s, but they were not representative of most of the work that came out of his shop.

*OPPOSITE: A trick entry in this section. The **Duquesne** is a 30-foot Ditchburn, similar to the **Wiggie III**, but three years newer.*

The *Wimur* was built for J.Y. Murdoch and delivered in 1927. Still in the family, it is the epitome of the basic, or we should say *classic*, Ditchburn family launch of its period. Nice and tight, with clean lines and good riding characteristics, and reasonably dry, with handsome and yet utilitarian hardware, it is a fine example of what Muskoka buyers wanted and what was produced by local craftsmen. The unique Ditchburn headlight used from 1923 to 1929, the wooden-framed removable windshield, the combination wood-and-metal line cleats, and the prominent deck-mounted horn, all spell a 1920s Ditchburn launch.

The *Wascana* was delivered in 1928, a year later than the *Wimur*, but exhibits the distinguishing characteristics of a Minett launch, compared to a Ditchburn launch of the same period. The unique double-hung windshield, the "Half-mile Ray"

spotlight mounted on the central post of the windshield, the distinctive bollard-line chocks fitted into the aft corners of the deck at the transom, and the transom made from a single plank of African mahogany are some of the details that make Minett's work stand out.

Earl Barnes learned his craft from Minett, and if he were an artist I suppose you could say his early work was of Minett's school. The *Algoma* was built about 1930 and exhibits many of the characteristics of the work done in Minett's shop. By 1929 Barnes had adopted the Indian-head crest as his trademark. The use of an ornament to mark the launches from a particular shop was peculiar to Minett-Shields, who used a stylized windswept lady's head as a deck or headlight figure from about 1927 to 1932, and Barnes, who used his Indian head a few years later.

*Opposite: The **Duquesne** was built in 1927, the same year as the **Wimur**, the 26-foot Ditchburn featured in this section. ABOVE AND RIGHT: Details of the **Wimur**'s Ditchburn look. Note the narrow interior mahogany-strip panelling (ABOVE LEFT). It was installed to cover the installation of sister ribs and other repairs.*

*The rounded transom and flare of the **Wimur**'s bow are clearly shown here. She is probably stained darker than her original colour, and her hardware is now chrome-plated rather than nickel, but that's nit-picking.*

A number of similar launches were built — many still on the

*lakes — but none prettier than the **Wimur**.*

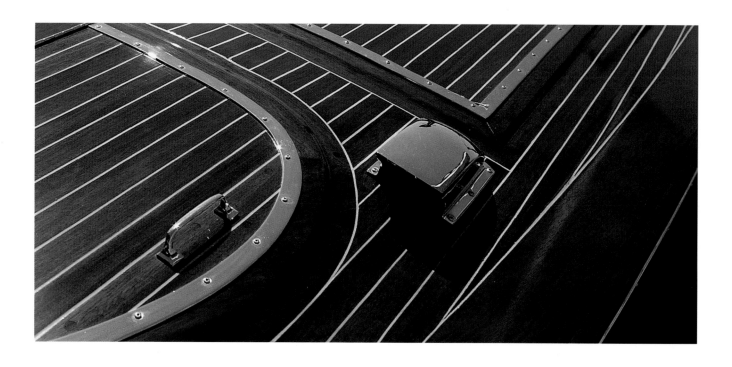

OPPOSITE AND ABOVE: *Here we see the* **Silverwing II**, *the Minett-Shields equivalent of the* **Wimur**. *Note the special double-hung Minett-designed windscreen.*

*OPPOSITE: The **Silverwing II** at speed. These launches ride so easily through the water that their speed is deceptive.*

*ABOVE: Two views of **Wascana II**, delivered in June 1928. Standard practice at both the Minett and Ditchburn works called for six coats of varnish on the decks.*

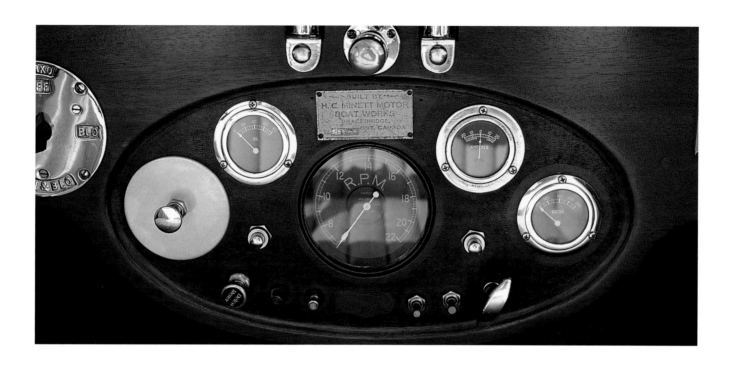

*ABOVE: The **Wascana**'s control panel. The builder's plate is a reproduction of one found among Bert Minett's possessions after his passing. This launch is really a Minett-Shields.*

*BELOW: A detail of the stern of the Barnes-built **Algoma**, seen idling* OPPOSITE.

*Opposite and above: Barnes's Indian head, mounted on the stem, became a well-recognized symbol from 1929 or 1930. The **Algoma** is another trick boat. She is not a displacement launch but has a V-bottom. She looks like a typical displacement launch and shows the direction in which some builders were taking the standard design in the early thirties.*

HARD-CHINE

HIBISCUS, ELSINORE, FLEETWOOD II, GLENAVY II, MARTINI

I n 1928 Ditchburn came out with a new, fast family launch that had a stepped hull. This new model was derived from the 38-foot high-performance patrol boats that Ditchburn had built for the Dominion government to control rumrunners in the Maritimes in 1927. This new standardized design was the first model to be named by Ditchburn – the Viking. The *Hibiscus* is one of perhaps fifteen centre-drive Vikings built by Ditchburn from 1928 to 1930. Hard, square lines spoke of power and performance, even when at rest. The long, raised engine compartment with its ventilators running down its length, stretching out in front of the driver, resembles that of the conventional racing boat of the 1920s; the roomy cockpit with

wicker chairs and leather upholstered seats recalls the family launch.

Minett-Shields built half a dozen hard-chine motorboats 24 feet and 26 feet in length between 1927 and 1930. Bert Minett had built at least one fast V-bottom launch in the early 1920s, again to a design by George Crouch, but when they turned back to building a planing boat, they purchased the bottom from John L. Hacker (George Crouch was by that time a vice-president of Dodge).

Ordered by Dr. R.J. Hutchison in August 1928, *Fleetwood II* was the second of the four 26-footers that Minett-Shields built. Apart from the upholstery, which was originally dark green, she looks exactly as she did when delivered on Victoria Day 1929. Still powered by the original 200-horsepower Scripps, she can make about 40 miles per hour – a couple of miles an hour less than one of the Kermath-powered Ditchburn Vikings!

OPPOSITE: A classic Muskoka scene — the **Hibiscus** *and the* **R.M.S. Segwun**.

OPPOSITE LEFT AND OPPOSITE ABOVE: A 27-foot centre-drive Ditchburn Viking. With stepped hulls and big Kermaths, they were the fastest thing on the lakes.

*ABOVE AND OPPOSITE BELOW: This 1928 Ditchburn 31-foot Commodore, the **Elsinore**, is obviously inspired by the new look introduced with the Vikings in late 1927.*

Between 1928 and 1933 Minett-Shields built four 26-foot hard-chine boats. All four are still on the lakes. The **Llan Llady** is still in her original boathouse; the other three reside within a couple of miles of their first homes. The **Fleetwood II**, shown here, still has the Minett-Shields ornament fixed to her forward navigation light. The company used the ornament as their symbol from 1928 until 1932. Many owners removed them and substituted their own.

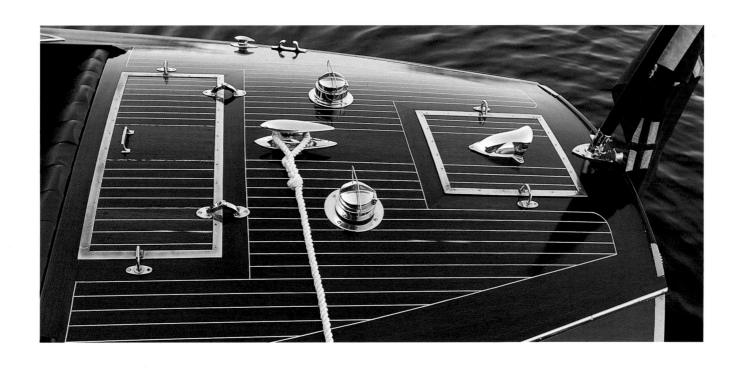

The **Glen-Avy II** is one of four 30-foot Minett-Shields launches built in 1930 and 1931. These fine examples of the boatbuilder's art incorporate a number of innovations. The inset navigation lights, forward navigation light set into the stem (OPPOSITE), and cast-aluminum transom frames (ABOVE), coupled with the traditional Minett preoccupation with the trimming and finishing of the deck, make for a satisfying big launch. Three of the four are still on the lakes.

*OPPOSITE: A very dry boat, the **Martini** is a 24-foot Minett-Shields that dates from 1932 or 1933.*

ABOVE: The flying of the Union Jack was, and still is, traditional boating fashion in Muskoka. Sixty years ago, articles appeared in magazines about the impropriety of flying the Jack at the stern. Many Minett boats never sported flags at all.

JUST FOR FUN

B-IV, Dix, Little Miss Canada, Shadow, Fancy Lady, Black Knight, Gold Fawn

One of the primary components of the boat-buying public in Muskoka was the "keen young man." Men such as Ewart McLaughlin, Carl Borntraeger, Dick Clemson, Charles Wheaton, Chauncey Hamlin, and Harold Wilson all wanted new boats, and they all changed their wants with each new development in speed-boating.

Carl Borntraeger was a motorboating enthusiast. Great excitement was generated by the outstanding successes of Harry Greening with his Crouch-designed and Ditchburn-built *Rainbow* in 1920, and Borntraeger wanted to be in at the beginning of the new scene. The appropriately named *B-IV* was one of a number of high-powered hard-chine planing launches

built in the early 1920s that were inspired by the Greening racing boats, and I believe that it is the only one that has survived the unforgiving vicissitudes of time and dry rot.

From 1921 to 1936 the little speedboats changed their appearance to a degree, but not one whit of their appeal. The first small production planing boat was built by Ditchburn in 1921 or 1922. Ewart McLaughlin's *Baby Olds* was a 21-footer inspired by Greening's Rainbow. In the mid-1920s Ditchburn came out with a double-ender that they built for Dick Clemson, the well-known *Dix*, still in regular use on the lakes. This design was modified by, among other things, the addition of a shingled bottom, and in its new configuration was now given a model name, the Rainbow.

In late 1932 Bryson Shields bought a third bottom from John L. Hacker: the first was

*Opposite: The 28-foot Ditchburn **B-IV** says it all! Seventy-five years old and still going strong - actually stronger and faster than ever!*

Gordon Finch's 24-foot *Glory II;* the second J.Y. Murdoch's 36-foot *Wimur II;* and this last was to be Edison Peck's 18-foot *Altair,* the prototype for the very successful 18-footers that are still so popular. It would appear that every single one of the six that were built from 1933 to 1935 was purchased for a 17- or 18-year-old boy. Edison Peck still has his *Altair* over on Lake of Bays, and Chas Wheaton the *Shadow* on Lake Joseph.

That same bottom was lengthened a few feet and a bit more beam was built in to provide somewhat more stability – not one of the more notable features of the early 18-foot models – and *voila,* the forward-drive sport hybrid. Not quite a traditional Minett launch and not quite a racer, but a handsome and satisfactory cross. The *Radio,* now known as the *Mab,* was built for Mabel Beatty, another of Bryson's ever accommodating relatives, who purchased launches from his works with a quite becoming regularity. Bryson kept the *Gold Fawn* for himself for a couple of years before selling to the Seagrams, who not only named it for one of their more successful horses, but painted the boat in their racing colours.

*Interior of the **B-IV**.*

It is said that Fred Gaby ordered the first of these "grown-up" sports boats, the *Blue Streak,* and that he instigated the new streamlined designs that made such a marked innovation in the styling of the forward combination hawsehole chock, and the combination rear flagpole receptacle and chock. The new streamlined mahogany engine compartment ventilators were introduced at the same time.

*The **B-IV** at speed. Impractical, but what fun!*

The **Dix** was built by Ditchburn in 1927 for Richard Clemson and after the war ended up next to the **B-IV** as a part of Cameron Peck's amazing collection over in Baysville. When the collection was auctioned in 1950, she came back to Muskoka. She was extensively restored in 1978.

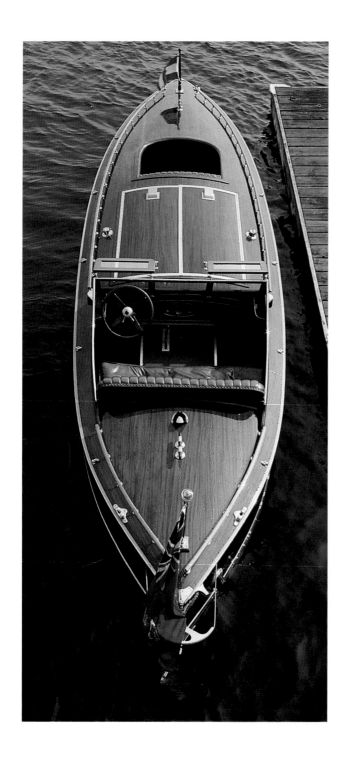

*THIS AND OPPOSITE PAGES: The **Dix** is built of cedar, though her decks are mahogany. She is powered by a Scripps Junior Gold Cup engine.*

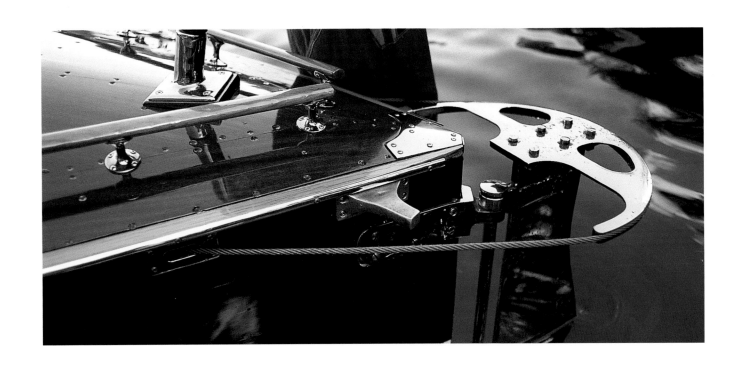

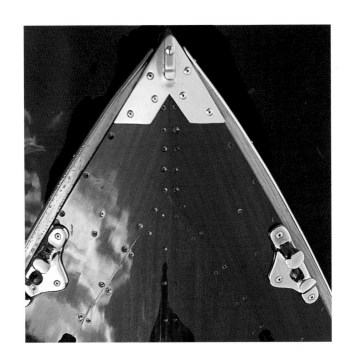

*ABOVE: If you confused the Minett-Shields-built **Black Knight** with a Greavette, you're not alone. Hacker sold the plans to Minett-Shields the same year he sold them to Greavette.*

*OPPOSITE AND RIGHT: The **Little Miss Canada** was the genesis of the 18-foot Greavette Flash. At least eight of these Hacker-designed sports boats were built.*

OPPOSITE AND ABOVE: *The **Shadow**, one of just six 18-foot sports runabouts built by Minett-Shields in 1933 and 1934. The **Shadow** is still the pride of her original owner, Chas Wheaton.*

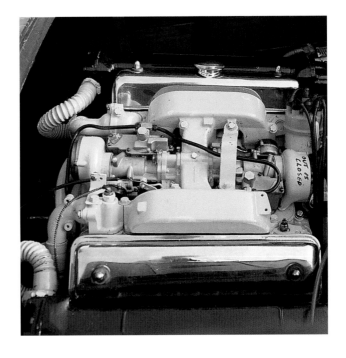

*OPPOSITE AND THIS PAGE: Minett-Shields 18-foot **Fancy Lady**.*

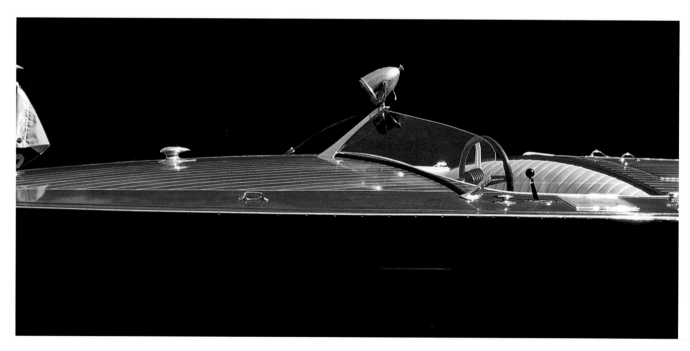

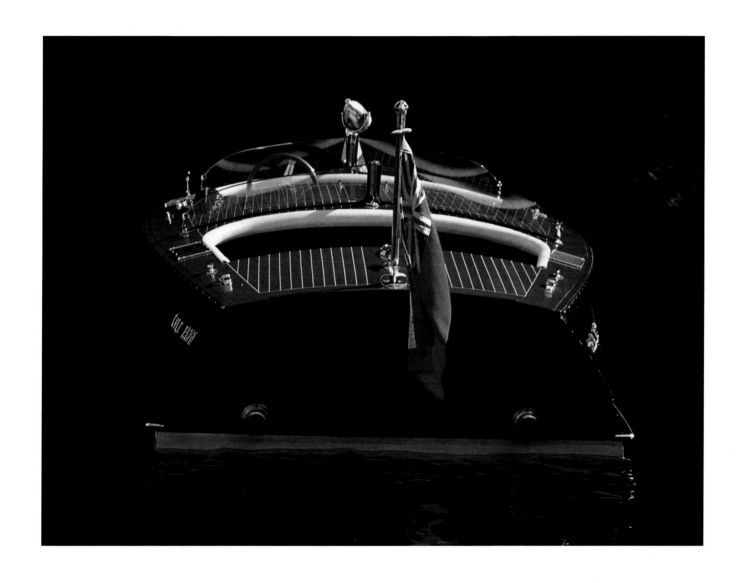

Opposite above left: The distinctive 1933-pattern Minett-Shield's ventilator was soon adopted by Greavette.

Opposite above right: A Minett-Shield's plaque used from about 1933.

*Above and opposite below: Finished in the Seagrams' racing colours, the 21-foot **Gold Fawn** is one of five built from 1932 to 1934 — all still on the lakes.*

NEW DIRECTIONS – THE NEW LOOK

CURLEW, MARJENCA, OSPREY III, ALZED, BLUE-B, DELTA

T he rolled sheer, the melding of the line of the deck with the sweeping lines of the sides of the launch as they twist from the stem to the tumblehome of the transom, says as much about the stylistic conventions of the thirties, with its obsession with streamlining, as it does about the consummate standard of craftsmanship that could translate those principles into a wooden launch. The concept was not new, nor was it introduced in Muskoka. Speedboats and custom runabouts were being designed in the United States by George Crouch and John Hacker in the twenties with this streamlined ideal, clearly inspired by aircraft, not motor cars. Chan Hamlin's 24-foot Minett-Shields, the *Hoo Doo*, built in 1926 or 1927, was the first launch built in Muskoka that adopted the rounded covering board.

*OPPOSITE: Something entirely different, the **Curlew**.*

Fred Burgess ordered a new launch from Greavette in the autumn of 1935, and they proposed building a 33-foot custom launch designed by John Hacker. Powered by a 325-horsepower V-12 Scripps, this unique launch, the *Curlew*, could make close to 50 miles per hour. Many would argue that the *Curlew* numbers among the most beautiful boats to have been built in Muskoka. It speaks of power and speed, even when it is moored at the wharf. It has a flatter crown to the deck and markedly less bulbous nose or bow than the famous Greavette Streamliners that were built after the war. The torpedo stern draws the hull to a more graceful conclusion than the flat transom that marked the basic Douglas Van Patten design used from 1938.

The *Marjenca* is another designer's interpretation of the standardized streamlined launch. The late Douglas Van Patten was a well-known American naval architect who worked for Greavettes in the late 1930s and for Minett-Shields in 1940. He reworked John Hacker's design for a streamlined launch, changing the bottom to a degree and adding more crown to the deck. He put his stamp on what was to become over the next twenty years the single most popular custom launch to be built by Greavette, the Streamliner.

Power boating and racing became increasingly popular in the 1930s. Motorboat races had been organized by the Muskoka Lakes Association from 1905, and these popular events became the highlight of the summer for many of the young and not so young. In the early thirties the nature of the races began to change as people started competing in boats that were designed as racing boats, rather than racing family launches, which had been the case up until that time.

The rear-drive 18-footers that were built by Greavette and Minett-Shields in 1933 and 1934 whetted the appetites of a number of young men, and they went back to the shops in search of something faster, something more exciting, something just for fun. The new 225 class was, for many of them, just the thing.

In 1934 two Ditchburn-built and Greavette-built boats raced at the Canadian National Exhibition in the 225 class. The next year a Minett-Shields-built boat made a showing, and a 225-class circuit quickly developed at places like Trenton, Picton and Muskoka.

Family launches had been raced at the M.L.A. regatta for decades and different classes established over the years. In the 1930s the principal classes were broadly defined in terms of horsepower: Senior, over 200 horsepower; Intermediate, over 100 horsepower; and Junior, anything under 100 horsepower. These new performance boats changed all that, and by the end of the decade the regatta saw a U.S. team racing a Canadian team. Many have said that this took all the fun out of the day. The regatta was never revived following the war.

It wasn't all just a question of high performance. As the boats on these pages attest, there were still boats being built that stood out in the crowd. They were hardly practical family boats but were definitely not built for serious competition. They were built for fun.

Marjorie IV, for the last 45 years known as *Osprey III*, was a one-off, built for the late

Marjorie Balm, whose brother Harold ordered a 26-foot streamlined launch with a torpedo stern from Minett-Shields at the same time. The *Osprey* is a bit longer, has slightly more beam aft than the Shadow, and a crown to her deck and a curved coverboard treatment that has more in common with *Norwood III,* built a decade before, than it does with the other 18-footers built a couple of years earlier.

Streamlined: the Greavette-built **Curlew**.

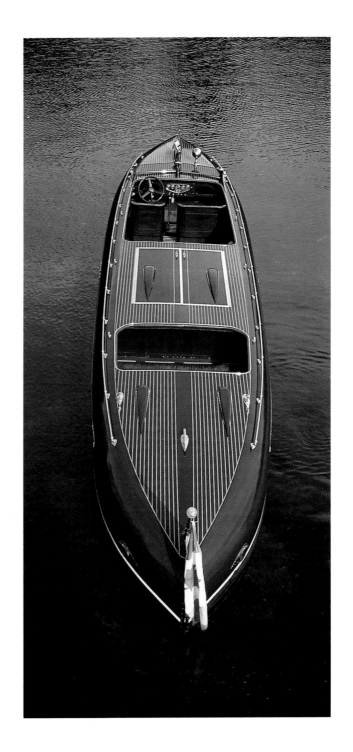

OPPOSITE AND ABOVE: *Built by Greavette in 1935, the* **Curlew** *is still considered by most of the old-timers — from all the different works — as just about the best thing that ever came out of a Muskoka boatbuilder's shop. Designed by John L. Hacker, she could go like the dickens, and ride well. To my eye, she has a pleasing "completion." You don't look at the* **Curlew** *and wonder where the rest of her is.*

OPPOSITE AND ABOVE: About seven or eight of these 24-foot Streamliners were built. Designed by Douglas Van Patten, the **Marjenca** *is a good example of the first generation of the launch that was to become Greavette's best-known model, though over the years it was reworked many times.*

OPPOSITE ABOVE: *A 1938 Greavette 24-foot Streamliner, the* **Marjenca**.

OPPOSITE LEFT: *From the mid-thirties to the mid-sixties, about sixty Streamliners were built. Most had cream-coloured bottoms.*

ABOVE: *Built with a single step, the 18-foot Minett-Shields* **Alzed** *looks better than her reputation. She has explored the bottom of Lake Rosseau a couple of times.*

These three shots of **Osprey III** show how Minett-Shields evolved, starting with popular 18-footers such as the 1933 **Shadow**. Built in 1936, the **Osprey** was a little longer, had a little more beam, and lots more stability! The covering board has more of a curve, is softer, and the front flagstaff picks up the curve of the stem — in the opposite direction of course! She originally had a green bottom and green leather upholstery. Otherwise, she is as was, same bottom, same sides, same boat.

The **Blue-B** is a Greavette Flash, a later version of **Little
Miss Canada**.

A curiously pacific image of a very hot boat (see page 60).

STAYING ALIVE

Hundreds of wooden boats still ply the Muskoka Lakes in everyday use. In this book, we have featured some of the finer, or at least the more distinctive, work that came out of the old shops.

Over the past ten to fifteen years, there has been a trend toward overrepairing and overrestoring vintage boats, to improve upon the original builders' work, to modify and reshape the original, and, in doing so, taking away some of the boats' distinctive character. The object in many cases is not to make the boat serviceable but to reflect the current conceptions of what a classic launch should look like. I think we should be wary of this trend, whose origins are a natural consequence of new owners' expectations and the current opinions of boat-show judges.

*OPPOSITE: Ron Butson's workbench with a half model of the **Vernon**.*

Ditchburn finally closed its doors in 1938, Minnett-Shields a decade later, and Greavette in 1978. The Port Carling Boat Works built their last production boat in 1959. Duke's sold their last production launch in 1972, and in 1987 built their last new boat, a replica of *Miss Canada III*. But many smaller shops now in business around the lakes repair and refinish old boats to a condition comparable to that of builders' work from the golden years. Launches are shipped to these small shops from across the province and from the United States. Butson's builds boats in the traditional manner, and their product equals or exceeds the demanding standards that we associate with early Muskoka builders. While busy with restoration and repairs, Duke's and a number of other independent builders have the knowledge and the capacity to build anything a boater might want.

In Muskoka, boatbuilding remains a living art.

Duke's shop. Boats have been built and repaired here for over sixty-five years. There has been a boatworks on the site for about ninety years. The traditional methods are still employed, whether in woodworking (OPPOSITE ABOVE RIGHT), mechanical installations (OPPOSITE ABOVE LEFT) or rebuilding (OPPOSITE BELOW).

*The **Executive** was the last all-wood model introduced by*

Greavette in the 1970s.

Here we see a new boat being built by Ron Butson, but the lines are

taken from the classic 18-foot Minett Shields Class E racer of 1933.

ACKNOWLEDGMENTS

This book is about boats, not people, but without the help of a great many people it could never have come to be. Over the past three years, hundreds of hours were spent on the water - in some cases in the wee hours of the morning - to get the right light for these photographs, to reveal the special art of the Muskoka craftsmen through these magnificent boats. We are indebted to a great number of very patient and cooperative owners for making this book possible.

In particular, we would like to thank the late John Black Aird, Kimberley Ascui, Doug Bassett, John Blair, Henry Butler, Ron Butson, Tim Butson, Hugh Boyes, Mike Campbell, Tim Chisholm, Gary Clarke, Lionel Cope, Sandy Crews, the Du Vernet family, Ron Firstbrook, Paul Gareau, Paul Gockel, Gerry Gonneau, Les Goodfellow, Jay Gould, Bill Grand, Jim Grand, John Grand, Stephen Grand, Ian Gray, John Gray, Dan and Joan Hauserman, Carl Herrmann, Toby Hull, Anne Duke Judd, Lloyd Koutsaris, Pete Lawrence, Peter Little, Lawton Osler, Nancy Muse, Earl Miller, Brian McGrath, Malcolm McGrath, W.F. McLean, Alf Mortimer, Hugh Munro, Mrs. Nobbe, David Pardoe, John and Keith Peck, Oscar Purdy, Rob Purves, C.F. Ross, Geoffrey Seagram, Ed Skinner, Robbie Sprules, John Taylor, Rick Terry, Eric Tozer, Michael Vaughan, Murray Walker, Charles Wheaton, David and Michael Willmot, Bruce Wilson, Gord Wilson, Henry Wilson, James Woodruff and George Wycoff.

We are especially indebted to Ian Turnbull and John and Pam Blair for making available to us their collection of old boating magazines. What pleasure this book gives is due in large part to the professional help of the editorial staff of Boston Mills Press and the designers at Taylor/Sprules Corporation.

OPPOSITE: What lies within?